*the*
# Diamond
*in your*
# Pocket

discovering your
true radiance

# Gangaji

Sounds True, Inc., Boulder, CO 80306

© Gangaji, 2005, 2007

SOUNDS TRUE is a trademark of Sounds True, Inc.

Author photo: Dan Dhruva Baumbach

Cover photo: Rosemary Weller / Getty

Cover and book design: Jennifer Miles

Published 2007

Printed in Canada

13  12  11  10

ISBN 978-1-59179-552-0

Library of Congress Control Number: 2005922173

# the
# Diamond
# in your
# Pocket

*For my true friend and husband, Eli, who relentlessly turned my attention toward truth, stopped my mind, and brought me to my final teacher, H.W.L. Poonja (Papaji), who blessedly revealed the radiance at the core.*

# TABLE OF CONTENTS

# PART TWO

# PART THREE

# PART FOUR

## CHOOSING PEACE 213

# FOREWORD

—by Eckhart Tolle—

"Know the truth and the truth shall set you free." These words spoken by Jesus refer not to some conceptual truth, but to the truth of who or what you are beyond name and form. They refer not to something that you need to know *about* yourself, but a deeper, yet extraordinarily simple knowing, in which the knower and the known merge into one. Now the egoic split is healed and you are made whole again. We could describe the nature of this knowing thus: suddenly, consciousness becomes conscious of itself. When this happens, you become aligned with the evolutionary impulse of the Universe, which is towards the emergence of consciousness into this world. No matter how much you have achieved here, unless you know this living truth, you are like a seed that has not sprouted and you have missed the true purpose of human existence. And even if your life has been full of suffering and mistakes, it takes only this knowing to redeem it and retrospectively endow the seemingly meaningless with profound meaning. If all your mistakes have taken you to this point, this real-ization, how could they have been mistakes? "I am not what happens, but the space in which it happens." This knowing, this living truth, frees you from identification with form, from time, as well as from a false, mind-made sense of self. What is that space in which everything happens? Consciousness prior to form.

Gangaji rightly says: "What I speak about has nothing to do with religion." Although at the heart of every religion lies "the jewel in the lotus," to use an ancient Tibetan Buddhist term, religion itself is not the truth but a story woven around the truth. Sometimes the story only veils the truth and it is still able to shine through it. At other times, it obscures and even usurps it. Whenever religion becomes divi-sive, as it frequently does, you know that the story has taken over. The essence that points to the underlying oneness of all life, has been lost. The story, of course, is thought, the conditioned, the time-bound. The essence points to the unconditioned, timeless, form-less, the realm of the sacred. "Be still and know that I am God."

For thousands of years, mythologies, that is to say stories, were the carriers of spiritual truth. Almost nobody was able to recognize the truth when it was pointed to directly. Most spiritual teachers used stories as their main teaching device. "All these things Jesus said to the crowds in parables, indeed, he said nothing to them without a parable." (Matthew 13:34)

For millions of humans alive today, the age of collective mythologies has already come to an end. Some substitutes lacking any depth, such as communism, were tried but proved to be short-lived and were quickly recognized as an illusion. All that's left now is each individual's private mythology, "the story of me." As Gangaji puts it: "Telling the personal story is the primary religion of most people on the planet." Where is the truth hiding in all those stories? When you wake up in the morning, you may remember your dream and realize: it was just a dream, it wasn't real. But there must be something real even in a dream, otherwise it could not *be*. What is it? It is that which enables the dream or the story, the thought or emotion, to be. This is the consciousness that you are.

Stories that contain spiritual truth will continue to be enjoyed in books and films even by those who no longer need them. They also still fulfill a vital function in initiating a first awakening in those who would not have been reached without the story and its ability to pass undetected through the ego's defenses. The ego doesn't realize until it is too late that every spiritual story is ultimately about you.

This book is meant for the rapidly growing number of spiritual seekers who are approaching the end of their seeking and who are ready for the undiluted truth. As Gangaji puts it: "At this point in our human history, what was once reserved for the most rare beings is available to ordinary people."

This book contains the living essence of Gangaji's work with countless individuals over a period of 15 years. Gangaji must have listened to—and cut through—thousands of personal mythologies (stories) during this time, but you won't find any of them here. Instead, you are given the means, through question and investigation, of cutting through your own story, the mental constructs that make up your conceptualized reality.

Except for the brief account of Gangaji's own story and how it came to an end, and the story about the diamond that gives the book its title, this book contains no stories and has no need for them. The words themselves are charged with extraordinary aliveness and transformative power. This is because they have come out of a living realization of the truth, rather than the accumulated knowledge of the mind.

This book is not only about the transcendence of compulsive and unconscious thinking and the end of human suffering. It is part of an evolutionary transformation of cosmic magnitude: the awakening of consciousness out of the dream of identification with form, the dream of separation. The fact that you are reading these words means that it is your destiny to be an essential part of this great adventure of collective awakening.

# EDITOR'S PREFACE

*The Diamond in Your Pocket* is a compilation of edited excerpts gleaned from conversations with Gangaji in public meetings and retreats since 1990. It has come into form in response to what Gangaji has found to be the primary concerns of the majority of people she has spoken with. These concerns revolve around the search for true happiness and fulfillment, and the understanding and resolution of the experience of suffering, both personal and planetary.

The root cause of all human suffering is one simple yet profoundly tragic mistake: the ignorance of our true nature. When we misidentify ourselves as separate egos, as individuals separate from the one source that animates all of life, we suffer untold misery and confusion. We are disconnected from each other and from ourselves. Whether consciously or unconsciously, we don't trust life. We feel alone and afraid and exhausted from frantically searching for self-confirmation in all the wrong places. This book is about the end of that search. It is about the immediate and direct possibility of discovering within your own heart an eternal wellspring of true peace and lasting fulfillment.

Within these pages is the possibility of realizing the final and absolute truth of who you are. In her many years of speaking with people around the globe, Gangaji's direct experience has been that even the most ordinary person—meaning every reader of this book—can immediately awaken to this truth of truths.

"Truth," as it is referred to in these pages, is the one core truth found at the heart of every culture and religion, the one core truth that all the great saints and mystics have pointed to throughout time, the truth of unconditional peace and freedom that lives in the heart of every human being—the truth of the essential self.

The chapters are woven together from many diverse conversations. As the book unfolds, the reader is led on an ever-deepening path of self-discovery. Gangaji uses myriad doorways common to everyone's life experience to point to the ultimate fulfillment that is simply waiting for our attention, waiting for us to stop and sincerely inquire into the deepest truth of ourselves.

You will find certain words and phrases used frequently throughout the book. Please excuse any redundancy. The intention is not to wear the mind down with repetition. Each mention is a fresh opportunity to discover the one immaculate truth in the core of your very own heart.

It is best not to cling to the words with the usual strategies of learning, because the mystery of the awakening heart is beyond the capacity of any mind to apprehend. But if you will just open your mind, it is possible you will experience an inner resonance, a quickening of the heart; and this spark of recognition has the potential to intensify into a raging wildfire of self-recognition.

*The Diamond in Your Pocket* comprises four essential themes: Part I, *The Invitation: Discovering the Truth of Who You Are,* welcomes you into the secret of direct self-inquiry and the possibility of discovering the deepest truth of who you are. It is an opportunity to recognize that whatever story you are telling about yourself, it is never the truth of yourself; that whoever you *think* you are, it is not the reality of who you are. When the activity of thought is stopped, even for an instant, the peace that is always present reveals itself to be the essence of all being.

Part II, *Beyond the Mind, Deeper than Emotion,* discusses the tendency to search for truth or fulfillment in our minds with the usual ways of understanding. It explores the avenues by which we identify with thoughts and emotions as if they are reality. When the voice of the ego/superego, which normally consumes our attention and directs our choices in life, is exposed as counterfeit, the true knowing of the heart is freed. We have an opportunity to discover that when any concept or emotion is honestly and directly examined, it miraculously loses authority over our happiness. Direct self-inquiry is the key.

Part III, *Unraveling the Knot of Suffering*, addresses the underlying causes of personal suffering. It explores the mechanisms by which thought and emotion feed into each other in endless cycles of suffering and confusion, all in the attempt to escape discomfort. The conditioned beliefs we hold about ourselves and the habit and futility of searching outside ourselves for happiness are investigated in depth. The opportunity here is to consciously examine the suffering inherent in the mind's ceaseless activities of running toward pleasure and away from pain.

Part IV, *Choosing Peace*, presents the possibility of living our lives as a clear and conscious reflection of our true nature. It asks us to take responsibility for our own experience of separation, to recognize that the suffering being played out on the world stage is no different from the suffering being perpetuated within our own minds. World suffering is only a reflection of our own collective inner state. Once misidentification is clearly recognized as the root cause of all personal suffering, then it is equally clear that the choice is to continue the indulgence or to stop. It is possible in any moment to choose peace, to choose surrender, to choose the inherent truth of the deepest knowing. The final chapters of the book give you the opportunity to discover doubtless self-integrity and the possibility of living a life in true freedom. You have the freedom and responsibility to meet everything openly and with curiosity and the freedom to live being yourself.

Throughout the book, Gangaji poses questions to encourage profound, honest self-investigation. It is important to answer them quickly so that the inner censor is bypassed. Their purpose is to create an opening for direct self-inquiry so that you can explore deeply within yourself the concepts and beliefs you have assumed to be reality, and which until now may have gone unexamined. It is my recommendation that you make the fullest use of these opportunities and the depths of realization to which they might lead. When a question is posed, you can close the book and repeatedly inquire into yourself, letting the answers flow freely, unedited. You might find it beneficial to write your answers down, keeping an ongoing journal of self-inquiry.

The questions are designed to evoke the deepest self-discovery, to allow you to see clearly what perhaps has not been seen, to tell the truth, and then to tell the deeper truth under that. The purpose of self-inquiry is not to "fix" anything, but rather to honestly investigate what is really running our lives.

Allowing the answers to come forth simply, honestly, and truthfully exposes the underlying beliefs that perpetuate personal suffering.

Self-inquiry is one of the most important messages of this book. By the time you are finished you will have tasted deeply of the power, simplicity, and aliveness of direct inquiry, and how it can easily be related to every circumstance in your life. When the light of conscious awareness is allowed to penetrate any story of ego-based suffering, the story cannot continue its position as authority over life.

As you read these pages, may you discover the absolute sweetness of your own innate being. May you look to where Gangaji is pointing and see what remains perfectly unchanged throughout every shifting circumstance in your life. This pristine sky of limitless awareness is your true refuge, it is love itself, and it is calling to you right now from the depths of your very own heart. Heed the call!

Shanti Einolander
Ashland, Oregon
November 2004

# ACKNOWLEDGMENTS

Deep gratitude to all those who have attended the meetings of the past fifteen years, for their questions and observations, which always point to ever deepening self-recognition; to the Gangaji Foundation with Manju at its helm, for tending this lineage of self-inquiry; to Shanti, for her tireless editing of the transcripts and her vision for this book; to Tami and Matt, for seeing the possibility.

# INTRODUCTION

T his book has arisen from fifteen years of speaking with people around the world—those in search of spiritual enlightenment, those seeking answers to the current climate of separation and war on our planet, and those simply looking for solutions to their personal suffering.

Until I met my teacher in 1990, my life was preoccupied with my own personal story of suffering. Although I was fed, sheltered, and educated by my parents in a relatively safe environment, I perceived myself as lacking, as needing something that hadn't been given.

I was brought up in a small town in Mississippi, with all the freedom and privilege of a white child of the middle class, yet I was secretly tortured by my family dynamic and shamed by my parents' alcoholism. I had the sense that I was involved in a huge mistake, that some force of darkness was surrounding me on all sides. The

Christian religious instruction I received did little, ultimately, to dispel this sense. In fact, it was amplified by the fear of everlasting hell for my inadequacy. For a brief time, I took refuge in the love of Christ, and throughout my entire childhood, the generous, unqualified love of my grandmother, Mammy, was the light that revealed the sanity and peace of the heart. Yet my childhood was not a happy one.

As a young woman, I married a wonderful doctor and gave birth to a beautiful, healthy child. Yet again, I was struck by the unhappiness that even my better circumstances could not dispel. What was the problem? I concluded that it must be me, so I began a search, exploring many avenues to correct what I thought was *me,* to improve *me,* to finally fix *me.*

By the time I came face to face with my teacher, I had worked on myself quite a lot. I had worked on my personality, my emotions, and my neuroses, and was relatively successful in those realms. However, I was still aware that I was living my life on a ground of suffering. I had tried many avenues to alleviate this sense of suffering—psychotherapy, affirmations, meditation, various workshops, channelers, astrology, visualization, automatic writing, dancing, psychotropic substances, acting out all my desires, and repressing all my desires. I had tried loving myself, and I had tried hating myself. None of it worked. There had been some beautiful moments, of course—

moments of grace, joy, bliss, and peace. But a thread of suffering ran through it all. Negativity and strife continued to arise within my own mind, and I continued to see it arise in those around me.

At that point in time, I had a wonderful life by all the usual measures. I was deeply in love with my second husband, Eli. We had a lively and passionate meeting on all levels. I had a daughter who was happy with her life. My health was okay. My finances were better than most people's. I had a career I believed in and loved. *Still,* I sought more; I feared losing what I had; I alternately hoped for and dreaded what the future might hold. It was exhausting! I became deeply disillusioned with myself and with the constant, everyday attention I placed on trying to fix myself. I had come to realize that there was a certain cycle to my self-involvement. At one end of the cycle was a sense of personal satisfaction, of the rightness of life's unfolding. At the other end were feelings of impending doom, an underlying experience of misery, and a belief in the hopelessness of the plight of the entire universe.

After a cycle goes around millions of times, it begins to get very familiar. The thoughts, images, emotions, and conclusions that were appearing had all appeared before. The jealousy, the envy, the seeking for experiences of gratification—at first sensual and intellectual, then finally spiritual—all led me back to my personal version of dissatisfaction.

Even as I recognized that my "story" differed from some people's stories, and was similar to others', I still believed it, and my suffering continued. Even as I recognized the tragically romantic story that overlaid most events in both my inner and outer life, I had no idea that this story was not actually *real*.

I didn't know what to do. How was it possible to be relatively happy, even deeply fulfilled at times, and yet continue to have a deep longing for something I couldn't even name? I had tried everything I knew to unravel this psychological knot of suffering.

Finally, I recognized that I needed help. I needed a teacher. So, I prayed for a true teacher, a real teacher, a final teacher—having no idea what a true teacher was, what a true teaching was, or what the result would be. I simply knew that I wanted to be free of the struggle. I wanted to realize the truth of my existence, but I didn't know how to do that. I recognized that I had tried every avenue I knew, and I finally gave up.

Within just six months of praying for a true teacher, through a miraculous set of circumstances, I found myself in India, face to face with H.W.L. Poonja (Papaji). He greeted me in a most extraordinary way. Eyes flashing, he invited me to come in and take whatever he could give me. He did not check my credentials; he did not check my karma; he did not tally up any merits. He saw in my eyes that I was thrilled to see him, and he said, "Tell me what it is you want."

I told him, "I want freedom. I want to be free of all my entanglements and misconceptions. I want to know if final, absolute truth is real. Tell me what to do."

First he said, "You are in the right place!" Then he said, "Do nothing. Your whole problem is that you continue doing. Stop all your doing. Stop all your beliefs, all your searching, all your excuses, and see for yourself what is already and always here. Don't move. Don't move toward anything, and don't move away from anything. In this instant, be still."

I didn't know what he meant, because I *was* sitting still. Then I realized that he was not speaking of physical activity. Instead, he was directing me to stop all mental activity.

I could hear the doubts in my mind, the fears that if I didn't think, I wouldn't care for my body, I wouldn't get up out of bed, I wouldn't be able to drive the car, I wouldn't go to work—I was terrified. I felt that if I stopped searching, I might lose all the ground I thought I had covered in my search. I might lose some of what I felt I had attained.

But he was a huge presence, and in that moment of looking into his eyes, I recognized a force, a clarity, and a vastness that stopped me in my tracks. I had asked for a teacher, and luckily at that moment, I had the good sense to pay attention to the teacher I had asked for. In the spirit of investigation, I was willing in that moment to stop following and believing in the thoughts beneath my doubt and terror. As I fell into what initially seemed like an abyss of hopeless despair, the fulfillment and peace I was searching revealed themselves to be here, to have always been here, with no possibility of ever leaving. Most shocking, I saw that I had always known it! In that instant, I realized that everything I could ever have wanted was already here as the ground of pure, eternal being. All of the suffering I had called "me" or "mine" had actually taken place in shining pure beingness! Most important, I saw that the truth of who I am *is* this beingness. This same beingness is present everywhere, in everything, visible and invisible.

In this realization, there occurred a remarkable shift of attention from my *story* of being to the endless depth of being that had always existed underneath the story. What peace! What rest! I had previously experienced moments of cosmic unity or sublime bliss, but this was of a different order. It was a sober ecstasy, a moment of recognizing, *I am not bound by the story of "me"!*

The simplicity of what I realized in that moment was difficult to believe. I had thought that it couldn't be so simple. I had always been taught that unless you are free of sin, greed, aggression, hate, and karma, you can't reach this place, and I had believed what I had been taught. Finally, I realized that *whatever* I thought was always only a thought, impossible to rely on because it was subject to conditioning and disappearance. In the discovery of truth, thought could no longer be trusted. Thought could no longer be the master. The previous fear of not knowing was transformed into the joy of not knowing. To *not know* was the opening of my mind to what could not be perceived by thought. What relief! What profound release!

After I had spent some time with Papaji, after he had questioned me and tested me, he saw that my thoughts had indeed stopped. When he saw the results of that stopping, he asked me to go "door to door" and speak with others of my experience. I said to him, "Papaji, I truly don't know how to do that." His response was, "Good. Then you can only speak from your own experience." He gave me the name Gangaji, after the holy river Ganga (Ganges) in India, because I had met him on its banks and because I had appeared to him in a dream as the goddess Ganga.

Eventually, others were interested in what I could share of my experience. The gatherings quickly outgrew our living room, and I began, as Papaji had requested, to travel "door to door," holding public meetings all over the world and speaking with people from every walk of life.

When Papaji died, an interviewer asked me what Papaji had meant to my life. I answered, "Before Papaji, I didn't have a life. I had a story of suffering. There were moments of pleasure, even moments of bliss, but still a story of suffering. In meeting Papaji, I lost my story and gained life."

Since I have stopped searching for fulfillment in the mind or in external circumstances, my life is now lived on a ground of joy. There are moments of unhappiness, anger, and distress; there are moods that pass through; yet all is occurring on a ground of joy. No mood needs to be feared, no moment needs to be avoided. Finally, I see that all moods, all states of mind, all feelings, anything that is truly investigated, points back to the same source—that pristine sky of fulfilled consciousness that is the truth of who I am, and is the truth of who you are.

I have been asked if I am a guru or the head of a church or religion. I do not think of myself as a guru, and I am definitely not the head of a church or religion. Some call me "teacher," but in truth I am no different from anyone else. We are all aspects of, or points of reference for, the one essential consciousness. I am able to play the role of a teacher only because I know that no role is finally real. The true teacher is alive within each of us and finally reveals itself in everything on the apparent inside and the apparent outside.

What I speak about has nothing to do with religion. Although my teacher's teacher, Ramana Maharshi, was a Hindu, and my teacher, Papaji, was raised as a Hindu, this teaching has nothing to do with East or West. It makes no distinction between Hindu,

Christian, Jew, Muslim, Buddhist, pagan, male, female, you, or me. It is the recognition of the omnipresence of being in which everything appears—you, I, ocean, mountain, and sky, all bliss and all horror. That field of pure presence is alive and intelligent and has the potential to consciously recognize itself in you.

The truth of who you are is consciousness: not your name, not your body, not your emotions, and not your thoughts. These are just coverings that come and go. They have a birth, an existence in time, and a death. Consciousness does not come and go. It is here now. It knows no other time.

Consciousness is free. It is not bound by any name or concept. It is not limited by notions of time or space. It is not affected by emotions or disease. You are pure consciousness. You have always been free, for you have always been consciousness. You have experienced yourself as a point in consciousness and, from that, imagined yourself to be limited to a body.

This recognition, even if it lasts only an instant, is the beginning of an infinitely deepening self-investigation. It is the end of preoccupation with the cycles of self-definition, and the beginning of true self-exploration that knows no limits.

To "stop" is to stop searching for yourself in thoughts, emotions, circumstances, or bodily images. It is that simple. The search is over when you realize that the true and lasting fulfillment you have been searching for is found to be nowhere other than right where you are. It is *here*. It is in you, it is in me, it is in all life, both sentient and insentient. It is everywhere. As long as you are searching for it, it cannot be found, because you assume that *it* is someplace else. You are continually chasing a lie.

The truth of who you are is utterly simple. It is closer than your thoughts, closer than your heartbeat, closer than your breath. If you believe your thoughts to be real, if you follow your thoughts as the basis of reality, you will continually overlook what is closer, what has been calling you throughout time, saying, "You are here! You are home! Come in. Be at home." To be home is to simply *be here*. To postpone simply being here is to engage in the infinite complexities of self-definition and misidentification.

Right now is the opportunity to stop and tell the truth about the flame of consciousness that is the essence of your being. To choose to deny it is to suffer. To choose to surrender to it is the end of all unnecessary suffering. When you meet yourself, when you love yourself, when you recognize that this flame of truth that you love *is* yourself, you have no need to search for love or to try and extract love. You are fulfilled.

At this point in our human history, what was once reserved for the most rare beings is available to ordinary people. Because we have considered ourselves ordinary, we have kept a certain door closed within our brains and within our hearts to the truth at the core of it all. But, at this time, there is a crack in our conditioning. If you are reading this, you are already aware of it to some degree or you wouldn't have picked up this book. This is a time of the ordinary awakening. This means *you,* not only those born under the brightest stars but the ordinary person as well.

It is my assumption that if you are reading this book, you must have some deep intention to be free, some intention to awaken. It is this intention that calls you home. It is the intent of this book to support the return of your individual consciousness to its source, the ocean of consciousness. They are never separate from one another in reality.

My intention is not to fix anyone or teach anything. Regarding the simple, absolute truth of who you are, nothing needs to be learned. The truth of who you are is closer than what can be learned. What if, in this moment, just as an experiment and in the spirit of self-inquiry, you put aside everything you have learned about who you are—including all your hopes and fears of who that might be—and open your mind to discover the *truth* of who you are? It is very simple. That truth is always here. My invitation is to stop all movement of your mind away from truth so that you can discover directly, for yourself, this jewel that is alive within you.

# PART ONE

---

## THE INVITATION:
## DISCOVERING THE TRUTH
## OF WHO YOU ARE

# THE LAST PLACE YOU THOUGHT TO LOOK

1

There is a story my teacher liked to tell about a consummate diamond thief who sought to steal only the most exquisite of gems. This thief would hang around the diamond district to see who was purchasing a gem, so that later he could pick their pocket.

One day he saw a well-known diamond merchant purchase the jewel he had been waiting for all his life. It was the most beautiful, the most pristine, the purest of diamonds. He was very excited, and so he followed the diamond merchant as he boarded the train, getting into the same compartment. He spent an entire three-day journey trying to pick the merchant's pocket and obtain the diamond. When the end of the journey came and he hadn't found the gem, he was very frustrated. He was an accomplished thief, and although he had employed all his skills, he still was not able to steal this rare and precious jewel.

When the diamond merchant got off the train, the pickpocket followed him once again. Finally, he just couldn't stand it anymore, and he walked up to the merchant and said, "Sir, I am a renowned diamond thief. I saw you purchase that beautiful diamond, so I followed you onto the train. Though I used all the skills of my art, which have been perfected over many years, I was not able to find the gem. I must know your secret. Tell me, please, how did you hide it from me?"

The diamond merchant replied, "Well, I saw you watching me in the diamond district, and I suspected you were a pickpocket. So I hid the diamond where I thought you would be least likely to look for it—in your own pocket!" He then reached into the thief's pocket and pulled out the diamond.

The treasure that I invite you to receive, that I will continually be pointing to throughout this book, is in your pocket right now, the pocket of your heart. The heart that I speak of is even closer to you than your physical heart. It is closer to you than your emotional heart. It is the heart that is the core of your being. Any step to go somewhere to *find* it implies that it is not already right here where you are. Simply see the radiant bounty of your true nature, accept that bounty, and then you will share that bounty quite naturally.

# SEARCHING FOR HAPPINESS 2

I n the heart of every human being I have spoken with, I have seen a command to somehow find true happiness, true fulfillment. Sometimes this desire is even stronger than the instinct to survive. As you know from your own experience, the search for happiness can take many avenues. In instinctive ways, it can be a search for pleasure, comfort, security, or a search for some known position in the herd of humanity. Usually, when we have accomplished some level of success in terms of pleasure, comfort, security, and position, we recognize that none of it truly satisfies this deeper command, this deeper call for true happiness. We may have moments of beautiful revelation, and certainly moments of pleasure, yet usually underneath it all is the fear that we will never find permanent peace or true happiness. Or our fear of losing whatever peace and happiness we have attained causes a tightness and contraction as we constantly try to hold on. Usually we feel a deep distrust that peace and happiness are really possible.

Sometimes, in a blessed life, there arises the call of the spiritual search, the search for God, the search for truth. We recognize that *the usual* means "don't take care of this command." We put aside what we have called "mundane existence," and turn towards spiritual life.

Unfortunately, the same conditioning that directed the mundane life usually attempts to direct the spiritual search as well, and it then becomes a search for spiritual pleasure, spiritual comfort, spiritual knowledge, or spiritual security. Sooner or later, you have to become disillusioned with that search also. You find pleasure, obviously. You reach ecstatic realms. You feel secure when you sense that God or truth is present, and are comforted when you feel held by that presence. But until you recognize that you have never been separate from that, you will continually thrust to find it somewhere, to find God, based on the belief or the hope that God will give you happiness. This belief or hope is founded on a pretty infantile understanding of what God is—some thing, some force, some place that can deliver everlasting pleasure, comfort, and security to you.

I have discovered that it is actually impossible to *find* happiness. As long as you are seeking to find happiness "somewhere," you are overlooking where happiness is. As long as you are seeking to find God someplace else, you are overlooking the essential truth of God, which is omnipresence. When you seek to find happiness someplace else, you are overlooking your true nature, which *is* happiness. You are overlooking yourself.

I would like to offer you the invitation and the challenge to stop overlooking yourself, to simply, radically, and absolutely *be still*—to put aside, at least for a moment, all your ideas of where God is, or where truth is, or where you are. Stop looking anywhere. Stop seeking. Simply be. I am not talking about being in a stupor, or going into a trance, but going deeper into the silence of your heart where the revelation of omnipresence can be revealed as your true nature. I am asking you to be still in pure *presence*. Not to create that, not even to invite it, but simply to recognize what is always here, who you always are, where God always is.

In this moment, however you are searching, stop. Whether you are searching for peace and happiness in a relationship, in a better job, or even in world peace, just for one moment stop absolutely. There is nothing wrong with these pursuits, but if you are engaging in them to *get* peace or to *get* happiness, you are overlooking the ground of peace that is already here. Once you discover this ground of peace, then whatever pursuits you engage in will be informed by your discovery. Then you will naturally bring what you have discovered to the world, to politics, to all your relationships.

This discovery has infinite, complex ramifications, but the essence of it is very simple. If you will stop all activity, just for one instant, even for one-tenth of a second, and simply be utterly still, you will recognize the inherent spaciousness of your being that is already happy and at peace with itself.

Because of our conditioning, we normally dismiss this ground of peace with an immediate, "Yes, but what about *my* life? I have responsibilities. I need to keep busy. The absolute doesn't relate to my world, my existence." These conditioned thoughts just reinforce further conditioning. But if you will take a moment to recognize the peace that is already alive within you, you then actually have the choice to trust it in all your endeavors, in all your relationships, in every circumstance of your life. It doesn't mean that your life will be swept clean of conflicts, challenges, pain, or suffering. It means that you will have recognized a sanctuary where the truth of yourself is present, where the truth of God is present, regardless of the physical, mental, or emotional circumstances of your life.

This is an invitation into the core of your being. It is not about religion or lack of religion. It is not even about enlightenment or ignorance. It is about the truth of who you are, which is closer and deeper than anything that can be named.

In any moment, in a split second, there is the possibility of recognizing the boundless, limitless, eternal, divine truth of yourself.

Experiences of truth have been given different names by different spiritual cultures. Heaven, nirvana, resurrection, enlightenment, satori, samadhi—all are names pointing to this supreme, unnameable, divine beauty, empty of suffering and filled with grace.

The recognition of this truth is all that this book is about. If you can't hold a word of it in memory, then that's just right. My teacher told me that the truest teaching is like a bird flying across the sky: it leaves no tracks that can be followed, yet its presence cannot be denied.

# OPENING TO RECEIVE 3

Opening to the truth of our own essential being is simply a matter of receiving. But because of our conditioning, this doesn't seem like a simple matter. There are usually complications and fears surrounding simply receiving, simply opening. We are conditioned to fear the unknown depths of ourselves, suspecting the worst. There comes a time when we can and must meet this primal fear. When we are finally willing to face head-on the suspected worst in ourselves, we discover an amazing, unbelievable truth.

Opening the mind to what has previously been feared and avoided reveals the capacity to bear and truly embrace discomfort and even pain. Eventually, the real discovery is that whatever we fully embrace always reveals the peace that we were seeking through all our attempts to avoid discomfort.

The capacity to receive is natural. When we are babies, we receive what is given. Unless there is some defect, this is the way the infant naturally forms and develops. Nourishment must be received for the organism to grow. Then, as we grow and our minds develop, we realize that receiving certain things actually causes harm: to receive food that is spoiled or poisoned is harmful to the body; to receive a parent's lack of love is emotionally destructive; for the mind to receive any indoctrination that teaches hate is brainwashing. Gradually we gain the insight that it is not useful to receive everything that is offered; from that, discriminating wisdom is born.

In the world we live in, much of what is offered is not useful, and it is often potentially poisonous. As we recognize the possibility of harm, we can shut down our natural capacity to receive. Along with the eventual and essential recognition that our parents and our world are not as benevolent as we envisioned them to be comes a huge disillusionment regarding our capacity to innocently open and trust.

As we grow up, we experience that even our friends can betray us, can lie to us. We experience in ourselves the capacity to lie to our friends, our husbands, our wives, our teachers, and our governments. We find that our own thoughts can deceive us or torture us; they aren't trustworthy. Our own emotions can get out of control. Our bodies cannot be trusted: they stumble and fall, they get sick, they age, and they die. The message becomes not to trust, not to open; opening is dangerous; it can lead to hurt. And with that conviction, a kind of hyper-vigilance of the mind develops to try to collect enough information so that if there is ever a time when it is safe to open, we will know when that time is. In service to this fear, most of our mental activity is concerned with collecting. No matter how much is collected, there is still more to collect. We go to teacher after teacher, training after training, book after book, tape after tape, in a frantic effort to collect the information we think we need to stay safe. Throughout it all, we have a profound yearning just to be open. This is often phrased as the yearning to "return home," to return to the innocence of a child, to enter heaven. But by this time, our mind is no longer a child's mind. Our mind, our body, and our emotions have experienced some very rough events.

Maybe in a moment of grace, you open to your wife or your husband, your child, your lover, or your teacher. But then the habit to close arises very quickly because memory, whether conscious or unconscious, reminds you that hurt can follow opening.

I am not suggesting that you *try* to open, or that you *try* to forget about the past, or that you *try* to receive. That will only create more struggle. What you *can* do is simply to observe when your mind is open and when it is closed. You can observe those times when you are open to receive and when you are rejecting out of habit. Simply tell the truth—not as a means of gathering more information, but as a path of self-discovery.

Telling the truth about any feeling, thought, or circumstance lays the ground for the power of self-inquiry. Inquiry is like shining a light into a basement where a creaky old furnace that you never even knew existed is spewing noxious gases all through the house. Inquiry opens the door and shines a light in the basement, so you can see and realize, "Oh my God, no wonder I feel sick in body, mind, and spirit." In that recognition, without even thinking, the natural course is to turn the furnace off. That comes from your own innate intelligence. You also see that you have within you an endless capacity to open the window of your mind and receive the freshness of what is truly pure. Along the way, you recognize that even with the experience of wounding and damage, a purity of being remains. The core of yourself is still whole, no matter what fragmenting has gone on around it.

It is not that people won't betray you. It is not that your heart won't break again and again. Opening to whatever is present can be a heartbreaking business. But let the heart break, for your breaking heart only reveals a core of love unbroken.

To open your mind to the silence that is the source of your mind is to open to your true self. Conscious silence is already open. *You* are already open. Allow your mind to stop gathering information, to stop imagining the future, and to stop strategizing for survival. Let your mind simply be held by its source. Recognize that the capacity to open to the truth of your being is always here.

Whatever question arises for you as you read this book, the most immediate answer to that question is simply to open. You do not need to understand the words. Just open your mind to where the words are pointing. The open mind reveals the open heart.

If you find opening difficult, you can examine whatever "story" makes vulnerability seem difficult. It's possible that you believe a story about how you cannot or should not open. The truth is that nothing is easier than opening. This may sound simplistic or abstract, but it can be concretely actualized every moment of your life.

In the instant of simply opening, you experience that whatever you were struggling with is no longer there. True openness reveals that the struggle—the problem, the bogeyman, the demon, the wound—is actually nonexistent. The story is not transformed by openness; it is revealed to be *actually* nonexistent. The only thing that holds the story in place is the resistance to opening. What remains, when what was feared or fought with disappears, is the openness of existence itself—the truth in the center of your own heart.

# DIVINE DISILLUSIONMENT 4

Another snag in spiritual investigation that must be unhooked and unraveled is the habit of looking for truth, perfection, or realization outside of ourselves. It is important to understand how this comes about, in order to unravel this very tight knot.

There is an exquisitely shocking and important moment in the course of your life when you recognize the habits, addictions, self-ishness, and suffering you have identified as "yourself." Along with this spiritual shock of recognition, a desire often arises to find what is true, real, pure, holy, and free. Because you have identified your-self as the negativity and horror, the search for what is pure and holy begins "out there."

We have many exquisite examples of "out there." We have sages, saints, messiahs, wise women, and wise men throughout time, whose lives we can look to and say, "Ah, there it is. They have it. How can I get it? Why can't I get there?" Then we make many attempts to fix what is now perceived to be disgusting and limited in ourselves, so that we can be pure and holy. We strive for that pure and holy image, we work toward it, we feel that we are gaining ground, and we find ourselves losing ground.

Finally, there is another great spiritual shock, which I call "the great disillusionment." It is the realization that all the work you have done—all the attempts to fix your character, personality, habits, and addictions—still has not touched that seeming gulf of separation between who you believe yourself to be and what you imagine to be perfection. This disillusionment gives rise to a spiritual longing, sometimes called the soul's longing for God. There is an understanding that all your attainments still haven't touched the depth of this longing. This understanding is crucial: you are recognizing that you will never be able to do it yourself because you don't have the power, and you don't know what to do.

There are many, many avenues leading away from this moment as you search for a way to fill that gulf of seeming separation. But rather than taking any of them, I invite you to fall on the double-edged sword of disillusionment and longing. Let the sword rip through your sense of separation. Refuse to take any avenue of comfort or hope or belief. Meet the sword; have it cleave open your heart.

Whenever this longing appears, dive directly into it: not into some story about the way out of it, but right into the heart of the longing itself. The disillusionment is a direct invitation into what it is you have been longing for. The acceptance of this invitation is rare. It is agreement to not move from the discomfort of the disillusionment, to neither dramatize the longing nor deny it, but to simply experience it all the way through. It is in this *radical experiencing* that openness is most relevant. By not moving in the slightest from the pain of this spiritual heartbreak, you can at last glimpse what is really here, who you really are.

The willingness to receive what is already in the core of your being is the willingness to not run from your own longing, to discover right now within yourself the source of that longing. Then you will discover that the longing itself carries you to the core of yourself, where true peace and perfection are revealed as never separate from the truth of who you are.

# WHAT DO YOU REALLY WANT? 5

One of the most crucial areas to investigate on the path of self-discovery is what it is you really want. When you come to the recognition that all the avenues you have tried in your search for fulfillment have not truly satisfied you, this question naturally arises: "Well, then, what is it I really want? If all the avenues I have tried in the search for happiness have not satisfied me, then what is it I finally, truly want when all is said and done?"

Most of us in the West lead extraordinarily privileged lives. Most of us do not have to worry about where we will get our next meal, or if we will have a place to sleep tonight. Most of us are not in imminent danger, and neither are our families. We find ourselves in a precious lifetime where we can set aside our mental habits and strategies of protection, and reflect on what is present when the mind is not busy being protective. In this moment, we can stop worrying about the future.

Obviously, everyone, even the most privileged, experiences some degree of suffering. But if you look out over the planet, you will see billions of human beings who are undergoing enormous suffering and who are almost totally bound by it. In contrast, the privilege of our lives is that we have the time, space, and opportunity to question the most basic assumptions of human life. We are free to examine our lives and to ask the deepest questions: *What is this life about? What is it being used for? How is my time spent? Where is my attention? Is my life meaningful? Am I happy? What is the longing of my heart and soul? Is it a longing for truth and freedom?* Most of us have the opportunity in our lives to fully consider the most profound unanswered questions.

In my experience of speaking with people, I have found that the discovery of what one truly wants can be a doorway to realizing true freedom. There may be an immediate response to that inquiry, such as "What I really want is a better life," or "What I really want is to be happy all the time," or "What I really want is the right mate." Whatever answer immediately arises, it is very useful to then ask, "What will that give me?" If you have the perfect soul mate, what will that give you? If you have a happy life, what will that give you?

If the answer is "Then I will be at peace, then I can rest," the truth is that this is possible now in this moment. Peace and rest have nothing to do with a mate. The peace, rest, and fulfillment you have been searching for outside, however exalted or sublime, are actually here now. If, in this moment, you can simply discard your outward reference points for what will give you peace, you might recognize that peace is already here, regardless of any internal or external circumstances. In this recognition, you can investigate more deeply to see if there is any separation between the peace that is always present and who you are. What is the boundary between who you truly are and peace?

What emerges in a perfect moment of realization is what has always been present, and this usually gives rise to a great laugh. What you have been searching for desperately, furiously, relentlessly, and with great frustration has always been present exactly where you are! It is present now, *in you,* and it can be revealed to you now as your own self.

What do you really want? I invite you to take the time right now to answer this question. Ask yourself repeatedly and directly: *What do I really want?* Let the answers flow freely, rising up effortlessly from the unconscious without censorship. There are no right answers. Consider these questions a game, a game that can expose whatever beliefs and concepts are still buried in your subconscious.

As you inquire within, let whatever sensations, emotions, and insights that arise wash through you. If you have discovered that what you finally want is peace, happiness, love, or enlightenment, now is the opportunity to see where you have been searching for them. You can investigate even further by asking: *Where have I looked for what I want? What activities have I pursued to get what I want? Where do I imagine I will finally find it? What do I imagine obstructs me from it right now?*

Are peace, happiness, love, and fulfillment conditional on some outside circumstance, or are they already alive within you? In this moment, be willing to tell the truth, which may at first be the relative, most apparent truth. For instance, your truth in this moment may be what you believe is necessary for your happiness. If your loved one is ill, you may be certain that you want only for him or her to get well, and then you could experience happiness. This relative truth can open the way to telling a deeper truth that reveals the paradoxical, causeless nature of true happiness, present now, whatever the circumstances. Tell the truth fully, whatever the cost, whatever the risk, whatever the consequences.

# WHAT IS THE SELF?  6

I nvestigating deeply into what you really want opens the door to discovering the truth of who you really are. If what you really want is to realize the deepest, core truth of yourself, then it is time to look more closely into conditioned ideas of what "self" is.

In our traditional Western understanding of psychology, personality is often used as an indication of who we are as individuals. But personality is actually a very superficial costume or mask that can easily be changed. If you want to change your personality, there are many books you can read, or workshops you can go to, or instructions you can follow.

There is nothing wrong with working on or changing your personality. It can be very useful. For instance, in order for human beings to gather peacefully in a room, it is helpful if their personalities have been conditioned enough so that there can be common courtesy and respect. This is all in the realm of personality. Working on personality doesn't cause any harm unless you somehow believe you *are* your personality. You may have already noticed that no matter how much you work on your personality, or how great a personality you have finally achieved, you are constantly frustrated in your efforts to discover the deepest fulfillment of yourself.

More primary than personality is a basic sense of ourselves as separate individuals, as separate "egos." What is the ego, really? Can the ego be directly experienced? Does it need to be eliminated or augmented in order for us to be happy?

Ego is the Latin word for "I." It is actually the thought of "I," a thought that couples with the sensation "I am this body," and from this starting point, expands into endless complexities.

In our experience of human incarnation, we have the natural capacity to identify ourselves as individual egos. This is an enormous power, and there is nothing wrong with this power. It is a delightful power, an evolutionary adaptation that has given the human species an advantage over other species in almost every circumstance. However, ego has also generated the root of all self-hatred, self-torture, self-love, and self-transcendence. If our individual body/mind/ego is believed to be our final truth, this belief subsequently gives rise to enormous, unnecessary suffering.

If you base your life on the belief that you are limited to a body, then both consciously and subconsciously, the preservation of that body becomes the overriding concern. In the growing recognition that there is no real guarantee for your body's safety, great fear arises.

The body is obviously subject to a multitude of attacks—genetic, environmental, and accidental. Finally, it is subject to the inevitable exhaustion of its functions. Obviously, any attempt to preserve and keep the body safe gives rise to strategies of self-protection or defense such as hiding or attacking. These strategies give rise to both aggressive and submissive traits, to social and sexual skills—all as a way of defending the thought "I am a body." This is ego.

When preservation of the body is primary, we live in a fearful and defensive universe. Defensive action—whether in terms of "me first," "my tribe first," or "my nation first," at the cost of all other people, tribes, and nations—gives rise to tremendous suffering. It leads to war. Whether this war is experienced between brother and sister, parent and child, husband and wife, or between tribes and nations, it is all based on a deeply limited identification of who we are, an idea of a particular someone who is essentially separate from someone else.

At a certain point, the reality of the death of your body and all bodies, all forms of every kind, becomes apparent. Although much of society, particularly in the West, seeks to keep this fact hidden, the death of the body cannot finally be denied. This demon death, which has been feared, denied, and run from, is called out of the subconscious to be faced in the light of conscious awareness. At this point, you can realize the undeniable presence of permanent, eternal awareness: the truth of who you are. This realization is the death of believing in the ego as reality, and the revelation of what is deathless. It is easily apparent that you are much more than a body. You are actually that which animates the body.

In final resolution, the ego is understood to be just a thought. Nothing has ever limited pure consciousness. The conviction of the egoic belief "I am this body" is, in fact, the only obstruction to recognizing the truth of who you are. This belief must be maintained hourly with incessant thought activity revolving around the image of who you imagine yourself to be. When you cease that thought activity, and instead turn your mind inward toward the central I-thought, you discover boundless, pure consciousness, inherently free of all thought and free of any need for safety. In this discovery, you understand that the ego is an illusion, just as a dream or a trance state is an illusion. It may be felt, seen, and experienced as real, but this is only because its reality has never been deeply questioned. This questioning is self-inquiry. Openly inquiring into illusion—in this case, the essential illusion—is the doorway to directly experiencing what is real.

When questioned, the individual "I" is revealed to be nothing but a dream. When you awaken from a dream, whether it was sweet or a nightmare, you realize it was only a dream. Obviously, there is nothing wrong with dreams or illusions. The problem arises when they are accepted as reality, particularly this illusion of the I-thought.

Everyone has the experience of being fooled by illusion—a mirage in the desert, or the horizon being the edge of the earth. Illusion holds enormous power until it is deeply questioned. True investigation is designed to reveal what is real and what is illusion, what is eternal and what is passing.

# YOU ARE NOT WHO
# YOU THINK YOU ARE

# 7

In our culture, we draw an understandable yet tragic conclusion based solely on perception. That conclusion is that since you and I appear to be separate, we therefore must be separate. This elevates perception to the position of authority.

The original sin, the original mistake, is the belief that separation from the source, from consciousness, from God, is even possible. Since separation is our experience, we believe it to be reality. This mistaken perception is the root of all suffering.

If you have been aware of perception for any length of time, you know that it is subject to change. If you gain just this fundamental understanding, which is quite profound in its simplicity, you have the opportunity to recognize that anything you can perceive is bound to be limited by the conditioning of your species, your culture or subculture, your family, your simple likes and dislikes.

The world is not as you think it is. You are not who you think you are. I am not who you think me to be. Your thoughts about the world, yourself, and me are based on perceptions. Whether they are inner or outer perceptions, they are limited. Recognize that, and you hear the invitation into the truth of yourself, which cannot be perceived or imagined, and yet permeates everything.

When all mental activity around who you think you are or what you need for happiness is stopped, there is a crack in the authority of perception, in the structure of the mind. I invite you to enter through that crack. Come in through that opening. When you do, the mind is no longer filled with its latest self-definition. In that moment, there is only silence. And in that silence, it is possible to recognize absolute fulfillment: the truth of who you are.

Any thought that you have had about yourself, however deflated or inflated, is not who you are. It is simply a thought. The truth of who you are cannot be thought, because it is the source of all thoughts. The truth of who you are cannot be named or defined. Words like soul, light, God, truth, self, consciousness, universal intelligence, or divinity, while capable of evoking the bliss of the truth, are grossly inadequate as a description of the immensity of who you truly are.

However you identify yourself—as a child, an adolescent, a mother, a father, an older person, a healthy person, a sick person, a suffering person, or an enlightened person—always, behind all of that, is the truth of yourself. It is not foreign to you. It is so close that you cannot believe it is you. Instead, you have taken on the conditioning of parents, cultures, and religions as the reality of yourself rather than what has always been with you—closer than your heartbeat, closer than any thought, closer than any experience.

The *truth* of who you are is untouched by any *concept* of who you are, whether ignorant or enlightened, worthless or grand. The truth of who you are is free of it all. You are already free, and all that blocks your realization of that freedom is your attachment to some thought of who you are. This thought doesn't keep you from *being* the truth of who you are. You already *are* that. It separates you from the *realization* of who you are.

I invite you to let your attention dive into what has always been here, waiting openly for its own self-realization. Who are you, really? Are you some image that appears in your mind? Are you some sensation that appears in your body? Are you some emotion that passes through your mind and body? Are you something that someone else has said you are, or are you the rebellion against something that someone else has said you are? These are some of the many avenues of misidentification. All these definitions come and go, are born and then die. The truth of who you are does not come and go. It is present before birth, throughout a lifetime, and after death.

To discover the truth of who you are is not only possible; it is your birthright. Any thoughts that this discovery is not for you—now is not the time, you are not worthy, you are not ready, you already know who you are—are all just tricks of the mind.

It is time to investigate this I–thought and see what validity it really has. In this examination, there is an opening for the conscious intelligence that you are to finally recognize itself.

# WHO ARE YOU? 8

The most important question you can ever ask yourself is *Who am I?* In a certain way, this has been an implicit question asked throughout every stage of your life. Every activity, whether individual or collective, is motivated at its root by a search for self-definition. Typically, you search for a positive answer to this question and run away from a negative answer. Once this question becomes explicit, the momentum and the power of the question direct the search for the true answer, which is open-ended, alive, and filled with ever deepening insight.

Of course, the external world tells you who you are. Beginning with your parents, you are told that you are a particular name, a particular gender, and that you play a particular role as a child in the family. The conditioning continues through your schooling. You are a good student, a bad student, a good person, a bad person, someone who can do it, someone who can't do it, and on and on. You have experienced both success and failure. After a certain stage, early or late, you realize that who you are, however that is defined, is not satisfying.

Unless this question has been *truly* answered, not just conventionally answered, you will still be hungry to know. Because no matter how you have been defined by others, well-meaning or not, and no matter how you have defined yourself, no definition can bring lasting certitude.

The moment of recognizing that no answer has ever satisfied this question is crucial. It is often referred to as the moment of spiritual ripeness, the moment of spiritual maturity. At this point, you can consciously investigate who you really are.

In its power and simplicity, the question *Who am I?* throws the mind back to the root of personal identification, the basic assumption "I am somebody." Rather than automatically taking that assumption as the truth, you can investigate deeper.

It is not difficult to see that this initial thought, "I am somebody," leads to all kinds of strategies: to be a better somebody, a more protected somebody, a somebody with more pleasure, more comfort, and more attainment. But when this very basic thought is questioned, the mind encounters the *I* that is assumed to be separate from what it has been seeking. This is called self-inquiry. This most basic question, *Who am I?,* is the one that is the most over-looked. We spend most of our days telling ourselves or others we are someone important, someone unimportant, someone big, someone little, someone young, or someone old, never truly questioning this most basic assumption.

*Who are you, really? How do you know that is who you are? Is that true? Really?* If you say you are a person, you know that because you have been taught that. If you say you are good or bad, ignorant or enlightened, these are all just concepts in the mind. All of them are forgotten every night when you fall asleep. Whatever can be forgotten will never deliver certitude. In an instant of true and sincere self-inquiry, what can neither be forgotten nor be remembered reveals itself as who you are. All that is required is that you stop trying to find yourself in some definition.

When you turn your attention toward the question *Who am I?,* perhaps you will see an entity that has your face and your body. But who is aware of that entity? Are you the object, or are you the awareness of the object? The object comes and goes. The parent, the child, the lover, the abandoned one, the enlightened one, the victorious one, the defeated one—these identifications all come and go. The *awareness* of these identifications is always present. The misidentification of yourself as some object in awareness leads to extreme pleasure or extreme pain and endless cycles of suffering.

When you are willing to stop the misidentification and discover directly and completely that you are the awareness itself and not these impermanent definitions, the search for yourself in thought ends.

When the question *Who?* is followed innocently, purely, all the way back to its source, there is a huge, astounding realization: There is no entity there at all! There is only the indefinable, boundless recognition of yourself as inseparable from anything else.

You are free. You are whole. You are endless. There is no bottom to you, no boundary to you. Any idea about yourself appears in you and will disappear back into you. You are awareness, and awareness *is* consciousness.

Let all self-definitions die in this moment. Let them all go, and see what remains. See what is never born and what does not die. Feel the relief of laying down the burden of defining yourself. Experience the actual non-reality of the burden. Experience the joy that is here. Rest in the endless peace of your true nature before any thought of *I* arises.

# TRUTH OR STORY? 9

Perhaps in that last investigation, you became aware of some of the stories that you tell yourself, or that your culture has told you, about who you are.

Storytelling is a wondrous aspect of human existence. It is used to address the whole spectrum of the human drama. It can teach, entertain, seduce, empower, and terrify.

Storytelling is the medium through which human beings express the infinite aspects of beingness. There are the stories about physical beings that can be touched, measured, and weighed: subatomic, microscopic, mineral, vegetable, animal, insect, vertebrate, invertebrate, planetary, and cosmic. There are stories about beings that can only be imagined, dreamed, and conjured.

Then there are emotional stories, the complex, overlapping, and ever-shifting winds of anger, fear, sadness, despair, joy, love, and bliss. There are mental stories, with beginnings, middles, and ends, with explanations and justifications. There are circumstantial stories, the interplay of the elements of fire, air, earth, and water with the physical, mental, and emotional influences of individuals, couples, families, tribes, societies, cultures, subcultures, nations, religions, classes, castes, planets, and beyond.

This inconceivable vastness of being is expressed through storytelling. Every culture, family, and person has a story with a past, present, future, hopes, fears, gods, demons, miracles, disasters, successes, failures, chaos, harmony, sublimity, and despair, from the highest caliber to the lowest.

Generally, every conscious moment of your life is translated and then placed into a personal story through the physical, emotional, and mental layering of illness, recovery, prowess, weakness, sexuality, procreation, status, power, conquering, surrendering, possessing, and losing. We are encoded with the cultures of Mesopotamia, ancient China, and the Holocaust of World War II. From the Sistine Chapel to the Mississippi Delta's juke joints, the story of beingness is told. History, remembered and forgotten, is the story.

What an extraordinary display! What exquisite and horrible beauty. The only element tragically missing in most stories is that which cannot be translated into the dimensions of physical, emotional, mental, or circumstantial. Yet this element is present in every physical, emotional, mental, or circumstantial event of any magnitude. The truth of what any story brilliantly and imperfectly expresses is the truth of beingness itself. The truth of *you*.

Are the stories true? Yes and no: yes as an account of experience, no as the finality of being; yes as an aspect of the totality, no as the totality itself.

# WHAT IS YOUR STORY?　10

D o you tell yourself stories? Are they stories of what you have or don't have, what you need or don't need? Are they stories of your freedom, your bondage, your lack, your bounty, your grief, your joy? Are they stories of who you are, of who someone else is? Are they stories of what needs to change, of what needs to stay the same, of what is right and of what is wrong?

Are you willing to stop telling your personal story? Are you willing to tell the truth about whether you are willing or not willing?

Whatever you are telling yourself, however horrible or grand, is a story. As a story, as a distillation of experience, it may be the relative truth but it is not the final truth. Stories appear, change, and disappear. Whether your story is about how good or bad you are, it appears and disappears. The final truth has nothing to do with emotions, biochemistry, or changes in circumstance. It is unchanging and unconditional.

You can stop telling your story in less than an instant. Even if it is a good story, stop indulging the telling of it, and immediately the truth can be experienced. You cannot experience the truth if you continue to tell your story, and you cannot continue to tell your story if you are experiencing the truth. It's obvious, isn't it?

Stop telling your story *right now.* Not later, when the story gets better or worse, but right now. When you stop telling your story right now, you stop postponing the realization of the truth that is beyond any story. All effort, all difficulty, and all conditioned suffering are in the resistance to stopping. That resistance is fed by the hope that the story will give you what you are yearning for, the hope that if you can just fix the story, make the necessary changes, you will get what you want.

When you stop telling your story about me, him, her, them, or us, you can know in less than an instant the true depths of what it means to *be* who you are. Then whatever story appears or disappears, it doesn't touch who you are.

When you dream at night, your dream has a beginning, a middle, and an end. It seems real at the time, but when you wake up you know it was obviously a dream. Similarly, you can wake up in the dream of your life. You can wake up before the story of you ends, as all stories will eventually end. Waking up *in* the story is called "lucid dreaming" or "dreaming clearly."

Normally, you wake up in the morning and pick up the story of who you are. You may do some meditation practice, but the real practice is the ongoing story of who you are. The energy and the emotion that the story generates gives birth to infinite permutations of frustration, delight, pain, or pleasure, all revolving around this practice of the story of "me."

Telling the personal story is the primary religion of most people on the planet. The personal story gets located in a body, a tribe, a nation, a religion, an "us." This is why the planet is constantly at war, and why you may be constantly at war with yourself. If you can recognize what your story is, then the story is conscious rather than unconscious. You can see what the story is, and you can choose to stop following it as if it were reality.

The possibility is to recognize that all our stories, however complex and multi-layered, however deeply implanted in our genetic structure, are only stories. The truth of who you are is not a story. The vastness and the closeness of that truth precedes all stories. When you overlook the truth of who you are in allegiance to some story, you miss a precious opportunity for self-recognition.

As a means of exposing your own particular story, you can ask yourself honestly and directly: *What is my story?* Exposing the story is not for the purpose of getting rid of it or following it. The purpose is to see what stories you are telling about who you think you are, or who you think you should be.

Whatever your answers may be, can you entertain the possibility that it is all just a story? It is not right; it is not wrong; it is not *real.* Experience the possibility of its unreality. Drop your consciousness back into the space where there is no story, where there is no thought. If a thought arises, see that it is just passing through. It is neither wrong nor right. It is just a thought, having nothing to do with the essential truth of who you are.

# SELF-INQUIRY
# EXPOSES THE STORY

## 11

S elf-inquiry is not the fixed question *Who am I?* Self-inquiry is a way of being, a way of living. It is the willingness at any moment to stop and ask yourself: *What is going on? What is being thought? What is being believed? Is it real? Is it true?* In this open investigation it is possible to recognize that whatever the story is, it is always only composed of thought. However strong the thoughts may be, however *relatively* real the story may seem, it is still just made of thoughts. Deeper than those thoughts, before them, after them, and gloriously even during them, is the truth of who you are. Without denying the relevance of any particular thought, it is possible to discover that truth.

Direct self-inquiry questions the basic assumption that you are "somebody." This assumption is rarely examined, because what usually follows is "what I need, what I want, what I have, what I don't have, what I should have," and on and on. These stories keep you identified as a person set apart from the vastness of your true identity. It keeps you identified only as a particular form, a body that is subject to birth and death. This identification is conscious individualization. There is nothing evil or even mistaken about individualization. It is natural in the evolution and development of the human being. It is part of the mystery of human beingness.

For most spiritual seekers, the belief that personal identification obstructs self-realization gives rise to the drive to get rid of the personal story. But this is still just another part of the story. It is so important to recognize this. Attempting to get rid of the story is just another tangent of the story, another example of the power of the mind to control.

I have often seen in spiritual circles that instead of a real examination of our storylines, there is a tendency to suppress the story. In that suppression, the story may seem to be removed, but there is still no peace. You cannot rest in the beauty and transcendence of yourself while suppressing the story of yourself. The story is still going on, but since you identify yourself as a spiritual seeker, you push it out of conscious awareness. Spiritual conditioning has simply taken the place of worldly conditioning. The story is still operating, but now it operates subconsciously. And you are confused as to why you still suffer. Continued suffering is proof that your story is still being told. If you are willing to not label that suffering as bad, then you can be willing to simply see what the story is.

# TELLING THE TRUTH

One expression of self-inquiry is to "tell the truth." I have noticed that people will often express a relative truth, for example, "I'm angry" or "You hurt me," and then assume that this is as far as it goes. The immediate, relative truth may very well be that you are angry or hurt, but that is not the whole truth. That is what you are *feeling*. What you are feeling in the moment may be the relative truth, but it is not the deepest truth.

Normally, we interpret what we feel, sense, and experience as the full truth, and our interpretation perpetuates the cycles of suffering. Our feelings, thoughts, emotions, and circumstances compose the personal story. The personal story is believed to be the truth. Whether the emotional story is one of anguish or one of bliss, it is not the final truth. To be able to distinguish between the story and the truth is an aspect of discriminating wisdom, which, in turn, is a natural by-product of self-inquiry.

Great confusion arises in our misidentification of who we are with the physical body, the emotional body, or the mental body. When the physical body experiences pain, we say, "I hurt, I feel bad." This is the common usage of language. Saying "My body hurts, my body is feeling pain" has a very different meaning. When the emotional body is in turmoil, we say, "I am upset, I am despairing, I am angry," rather than "My emotions are in turmoil, there is anger appearing, there is despair appearing."

Whether you are happy or sad, you have the opportunity to tell the truth about what is deeper than that feeling. This is radical for most people, because when they feel sad, they just want to feel happy again. For most, that natural desire is as far as it goes. Or if they are feeling happy, they always want to feel that happiness and never feel sad again.

The law of changing conditions is obviously a basic law of this planet. Every *thing* is subject to change—all objects, thoughts, feelings, states of mind, health, and governments—in short, every circumstance changes. Change is the law of the five elements of our universe. Change is the law of the weather, of the seasons, of the hours in a day. If those changing conditions can be surrendered to rather than resisted, then feelings of unhappiness are simply feelings of unhappiness. They have no more significance than that they are feelings of unhappiness. Following this recognition, you can experience them as you can the sun or the rain. You don't *always* have to have the sun; in fact, you won't. Whatever is appearing is just the way it is.

Every *thing* is subject to change. What is not subject to change? Your true nature. Whatever you think you are, see if it is subject to change. If it is, then as an experiment, discard that belief and tell the truth about what remains. What does not change with the changing of your body? What does not change with the changing of your circumstances? What does not change when your emotions change? Tell the truth all the way. Don't settle for a superficial, relative truth. Tell the truth all the way until you *know* yourself as *changelessly* present.

Telling the truth has to be even more important than enlightenment, more important than happiness. Through devotion to telling the truth, and then the ever deeper truth, your personal story in all its shocking dimensions is revealed to have no final reality.

To identify yourself as only a body or a passing state or condition is the root of all personal suffering. At the same time, directly underneath any experience of suffering, the truth of who you are lies waiting to be revealed. You are radiant, free consciousness. When radiant, free consciousness is obscured by the identification of yourself as only a body, a thought, an emotion, or a circumstance, then you are living a lie; and with a lie there is always suffering.

Many of us live our lives very superficially. We suffer for that superficiality, because within each one of us lives a depth of being that wants itself known, wants itself felt, wants itself expressed and met. As long as we settle for the superficial truths, we tragically miss the deeper revelation.

We experience a huge collective suffering on this planet, yet at any point, we have the full capacity to stop and tell the truth—what is here? Sadness may be here, anger may be here, but what else is here? What is deeper than that? At any point, we have the opportunity to direct our attention away from the future or the past, and toward this moment so that we can truly self-inquire into what is final, what is always present.

# SEE WHAT IS ALWAYS HERE 13

We all have the capacity to swim naked in the ocean of consciousness that is the true self. The true self is not *your* self. It is what your mind and body are *in,* what nothing alive can exist without, but which is limitless and blessedly exists without your effort. I say "blessedly," because if it depended on you for its existence, then you would have to make some huge effort to establish it, to maintain it, and to make sure that it didn't die. Generally, once people have tasted the nectar of their true self, this is what they get very busy trying to do.

The taste itself is a mystery to which we can apply numerous metaphysical theories, but the mystery continually defies all theories. The idea that the truth of who you are can penetrate your individual consciousness for even an instant and reveal what individual consciousness is made of, while remaining independent of individual consciousness, flattens your mind. Then the mind usually goes to work; it tries to retrieve that moment of absolute awe, or keep it, or understand it, or serve it—to generally *do* something with it. The mind makes many attempts to "keep" what is already always here, and these attempts feed the mind's activities of working to understand. Then one day, individual consciousness is finished. As the joke goes, "... and then you die." The ever-present possibility in your life right now is to stop trying to do anything to *get* who you are, and simply rest in this nectar of pure consciousness that is always here.

To try to keep what is always here is absurd. To try to establish what is already eternally established is ridiculous. That it is impossible is good news. The bad news is that in trying to keep what is already permanently here, the "hereness" is tragically overlooked. Because we base our energy and thoughts on states of individual consciousness, we constantly overlook the truth of stateless consciousness, which is always present.

Consciousness is not an object. It is *hereness itself.* Our minds are usually involved with an object that appears and disappears in the hereness, and because of that, we overlook the nature of hereness. Pure consciousness is what these words appear in, what this book appears in, what all bodies appear in. It infuses all words and bodies, and it is conscious of itself, and it is you. In your recognition of yourself as pure consciousness, you awaken to yourself.

Normally, when we speak of consciousness, we are referring to particular states of awareness—being aware of something or not being aware of something—rather than to the *awareness itself.*

For instance, we may identify focused consciousness as "awareness" and unfocused consciousness as "unawareness." Unawareness becomes equated with "unspiritual" or "not awake." But consciousness is fully present in each state. In one state, it is clear, aware of present time, with focused attention. In the other state, it is diffuse, unaware of time, and purely subjective. Each state, awareness or unawareness, is suited to different situations. For instance, if you are learning something new or performing a task that requires detailed focus, to be focused on the object to be learned or the task performed is more appropriate than being unaware of it. On the other hand, if you're spaciously reflecting, such as prior to discovering the solution to a problem or creating art, it is more appropriate to have no object in mind. It is more appropriate when embracing a lover or a child to be in a timeless, suspended state. In an extreme example, sleep requires suspension of objects and time, while driving a car demands focus on objects and time.

Different cultures and subcultures tend to elevate certain states of consciousness and devalue other, apparently opposing states. For someone conditioned by the corporate world, consciousness focuses on the "real world" of time and getting and keeping objects. Someone committed to this worldview may retreat from their real world for recreation, but it is clear to them where reality is. Likewise, most religions and spiritual movements place reality in what may be called "heaven," "nirvana," "paradise," or "transcendence." Of course, there is overlapping in all worldviews, but the elevated state is considered the ultimate reality.

However, if we stop valuing one state over another—even for just a moment—then we can discover that awareness itself is continuous and that all states move in and out of awareness. Awareness is unchanged by any state that appears in awareness.

This is a radical invitation: Do not try to reach any state of awareness, whether focused or diffused, and do not try to keep any state away. Rather, recognize what is always present. The wonderful result of this recognition is that objective states become clearer, subjective states become softer, and peace is found in all states.

While it is useful to develop your mind, your body, and your work, developing *consciousness* is a huge mistake. Development happens only because consciousness is already here. If your attention is on "developing" rather than on recognizing this, you go in a circle, chasing your tail and searching for what is still here.

In a moment of truth-telling, you can recognize for yourself, "Oh, I picked up the search again." You can deny that you have picked up the search, you can justify picking up the search, or you can stop. In that moment, you can turn your attention to the silence at the core of whatever is occurring.

I invite you to stop. Right here. Right now. Stop. Whatever it is you are searching for, stop. Whatever it is you are trying to keep away, stop. Stop and see what is always here. It may appear terrifying, it may appear thrilling, it may appear dead, it may appear blank, but if you stop reaching for it or running from it, you cannot help but finally see what *is*.

I use the word "consciousness," but if you have some idea of what that is, throw it away. We can also use the word "God," but there are confusing meanings of God according to each religion and even each individual mind. No matter how you have tried to name it, drop the words you have used and see what is left. See what is shining *here,* right now, without needing a name or a definition. For an instant, recognize not only what is within you, but also what you are *in*—what you are born into, what you live in, and what you will die into.

As a means of deeper investigation, you can inquire directly within. You can ask yourself this question: *What is here?*

Take a moment just to be still, to be here, regardless of what is passing through you. Recognize that *you are the hereness* that all is passing through. All the changes, sights, sounds, smells, emotions, thoughts, information, events, births, and deaths are all passing through the ever-present stillness that is here now in the core of your being.

# THE POWER
## OF STOPPING 14

S elf-inquiry is not a path that leads you somewhere. It is the
path that stops you in your tracks so that you can discover
directly, for yourself, who you are.

The power of stopping is indescribable. In the moment of stopping, there is no concept of anything, yet there is consciousness.
Consciousness without concept is naturally and inherently free. In
an instant, it is *self-evident*. We are so trained to follow our concepts
that we even turn consciousness itself into a concept.

In the timeless instant of recognizing that consciousness exists
without any need of concept, identification with concept falls away.
This is an essential experience. What follows is the deepening recognition that *consciousness is free* regardless of concept. This is true
freedom. The concept of yourself as a man or a woman doesn't even
begin to touch the truth of yourself as consciousness.

Fear is often a part of this essential shift away from identification with concepts toward identification with the silent ground of being, because the shift threatens the known structure of life. Fear can have many different disguises, including anger, numbness, and despair. This existential terror is like the gargoyle at the gate to the sanctuary. Unless it is met and exposed as just another strategy of mind, it can keep you away from the revelation of the silent, aware peace at the core of your being.

The great masters who have realized their essential nature encourage us to meet this terror of the dissolution of our individuality. The result of this meeting is paradoxical: the individual is dissolved and yet becomes more individually distinct. The uniqueness of consciousness is that consciousness can recognize itself through the individual form and simultaneously recognize itself as the animating force of everything.

There comes a point of willingness to surrender individuality. In that willingness, what is actually released is conditioned individuality, and individual consciousness reveals itself to be unified with *all* consciousness. Yet, first must come the willingness to lose everything that is perceived to be the individual self. Fear arises only because the reality of this loss cannot be imagined. When the loss comes, it is actually very good news. The individual identity is revealed to be the husk that covers the sweet truth of self-realization.

Just take a moment, this moment, to let everything go—the search, the denial, the rejection, the clinging. Let it all go and just for this moment rest in the truth of your being. Then whatever comes after that can be seen and experienced in the context of the sanctuary of beingness.

# RESTING IN NOTHING

15

As you read this, simply relax. In that relaxation, see if tendencies arise to do something, to make something of this moment, to either try to keep this moment or try to push it away. I suggest that all these tendencies are built around some kind of defense against the intimation and the deep self-knowing that you are really not an individual body, you are really not a personality, in fact, you are nothing at all. When "nothing at all" is interpreted by the mind, it is a fearful thought: a thought of death, of worthlessness, of being dispensable. Because of your deep identification with the body and with thoughts, this fear can be very strong.

Mind patterns of defense against nothingness, against emptiness, can be found wrapped around this fear. These patterns are strategic responses to fear. The mind may quickly become very active: "Yes, but what does this mean? This can't be so. How will I be able to do my job?" Just for this moment, let all those thoughts fall aside. Allow your mind to rest in nothing—being nothing, doing nothing, having nothing, getting nothing, keeping nothing. In this moment, if you can actually, willingly, consciously, simply be nothing at all, in a flash you can discover the peace, the expansion, the freedom from boundaries inherent in nothingness.

The truth is, you really are nothing, but this nothing is full, whole, infinite, in everything, everywhere. This nothing is consciousness itself. It is already whole, complete, and fulfilled. This is the amazing irony. What you are running from and what you are searching for are the same!

I know you must experience at least a hint or an echo of the boundless peace that is present. This is an echo of your true identity, which is always present. However many strategies of the mind arise—to do, to keep, to hide, to protect, or to defend—this boundless peace is always present, and it is your true refuge. This is, in fact, your true face. You do not need years of spiritual practice to find your true face, because it is always present. Nor do you need to be a better person to find your true face. Right now, exactly where you are, whoever you imagine yourself to be, your true face is shining. But it is actually no face at all, with no gender, no agenda. It is simply shining as it is, shining as shiningness.

I am often asked why it is we misidentify and cover our true face in the first place. There are many spiritual and metaphysical theories as to why, but the one that makes the most sense to me is that the extraordinary delight of uncovering the true face is made possible only by the extraordinary suffering of covering the face. Perhaps you can remember the thrill of playing "hide and seek" as a child. You can remember the thrill of hiding until after a while the thrill wears off, and then a desire arises for the thrill of being found.

In your life, if the desire to be found has arisen, then it is time to be found. It is time to stop hiding from the *concept* of nothingness and return to the *truth* of nothingness. It is time to rest in that. Then you will see that the habits of misidentification, the strategies of control and hiding, the conditioned beliefs in the necessity to hide, will all be exposed, leaving you free to simply be.

As an experience, the power of individuation is wondrous, and there is nothing wrong with it. But it is an experience of hiding. It is an experience of the whole disguising itself as the individual. It is now possible for the whole to shine through the disguise of the individual. All that is required is your readiness, your willingness, your proclamation, "Yes, now I am ready, really ready, to be found."

Of course, since you have been hiding for millions of years in some version of this particular genetic form, there will be enormous forces that will come and say, "No, not yet, not quite, a little later. This is not a good time." But I say yes, now, even when all these forces of the past are coming, this is the time to be found. Then these forces of conditioning become the fuel for a huge bonfire that lights your way home. Invite all of your conditioning to be exposed in the light of this fire, to be exposed in the light of real self-inquiry.

# PART TWO

---

## BEYOND THE MIND,
## DEEPER THAN
## EMOTION

# PEACE IS BEYOND UNDERSTANDING

## 16

As awakening starts in a human mind, one of the first events in that process is the recognition of the immense contradictions in life, of both the beauty and the horror in our own experience and in the global experience. This recognition is a shock to the system. Usually a desire arises to understand what it all means. Is it an evil universe or a holy universe? If it's an evil universe, then how do we get out? In this desire, the search for understanding begins. We may go to our parents, our teachers, our culture, and our religions for understanding, and we may accept or reject their version of reality. Either way, the confusion continues.

Amazingly, in some moment of grace, we know absolutely that we are one with the universe, that all is perfection. Whether it is a split second of simply looking into a baby's face or a longer period of abiding peace, we know it. And then, inevitably, other experiences arise of the horror or seeming meaninglessness of life. Again, we realize that we don't know anything, and the search for understanding continues.

I know this only, of course, because this was the story of my life until I met my teacher, who invited me to stop all searching. At that point, I felt that the search for understanding was supreme. However, when I really let that word "stop" all the way into my consciousness, I recognized that surely there was one second in the many seconds of this lifetime when I could stop all searching. That instant of stopping revealed the peace that is beyond understanding. In that peace, I discovered the inclusion of all horror and all beauty, all desperation and all relaxation. But that revelation did not occur through understanding. While moments of profound understanding occur, a lasting understanding follows the direct experience of everlasting peace.

Usually, we search for understanding because we believe that it will lead to true experience. We try to understand every experience that is brought to us, and then we have our little mental niches where we put the experience. This is one example of how the great power of the mind leads our lives. But when it comes to the recognition of truth, the mind is not equipped to lead. It is exquisitely equipped to discover or to follow, but not to lead. The mind is not the enemy; there is nothing wrong with it. The tragedy is that we believe the conclusions of the mind to be reality. This is a huge tragedy, responsible for both mundane suffering and the most profound suffering, individually and collectively.

You are conditioned to try to keep mental understanding in an exalted place, but that is not true understanding. That is in the realm of understanding how to tie your shoes, practice good manners, learn a new language, or decipher advanced mathematical formulas. The power of understanding, which is a beautiful power of the mind, is useless in the discovery of your true self.

Whatever you are searching for in this moment, however worldly or spiritual it may be, just stop. A huge fear may arise—the fear that if you stop, you will die, you will never make it to where you are headed. This fear is understandable, but all the magnificent beings who have preceded you encourage you to know that the mind's true stopping is absolutely good news. Deep inside, you already know this. You just can't quite believe it is true, because you don't understand it. And you want to understand it so that you will then have some control over it; it will have a place and be definable as something religious, spiritual, or existential.

To know what you know in the core of your being without understanding is effortless. The effort arises in having to understand it so that you can mentally know it and remember it, so that it will be there for you if you get into trouble. I invite you to stop that search for understanding right now and meet the very force that has fueled your search. To not move toward either rejecting or grasping. To be still, regardless of the fears, anxieties, helplessness, hopelessness, despair, bliss, thrill, or explosion of realization. Is it possible to simply be here, not understanding a thing?

Is there some belief that in order to survive as an individual you have to understand with the mind? As you inquire into the reality of that belief, you can discover that the truth of who you are, consciousness itself, already knows itself, is already in surrender to the mystery of itself; and in this realization, you know yourself even more deeply. Whatever understandings follow are secondary, even the most profound understanding of the unity of all existence. The truth of who you are as pure consciousness, the totality of being, is infinitely deeper and vaster than any mental understanding of it.

The effects of this realization can be quite exquisite, and there often follows some capacity to articulate it, as we know from holy books and scriptures. But once the thoughts are believed—"Now I know it, now I understand it, now it is mine"—the mystery becomes a concept, a story about a moment of truth experienced sometime in the past.

The simplicity of the truth is what keeps it out of the reach of any concept, including whatever concepts might be used in the moment to point to it. It is out of reach because it is too close to be reached.

Concepts of the mind are distant compared with the closeness of the truth of who you are.

At a certain point, you recognize that you don't understand a thing, and you experience a moment of surrender. The paradox is that, as soon as you surrender the need to understand, you do understand; and the moment you think you do understand, you don't understand.

In your willingness right now, in this moment, to relinquish all understanding, all that you ever searched for through understanding is revealed.

# THE UNGRASPABLE
## OFFERING 17

What my teacher offered to me, and what I am offering to you, is very simple. It has nothing to do with acquiring any special power. It has nothing to do with acquiring a particular state of mind. It has nothing to do with any qualities, not even warm, gentle ones. It is about what is eternally, undeniably, uncontrollably, permanently here in every moment, every second, every situation, and every state of mind. Everything that is graspable by the mind, even the most sublime and elevated states, has a birth, an existence, and a death. What is permanently here is ungraspable by the mind because it is not an object.

If you look into your life, you will recognize that this is true of every thought, emotion, conclusion, self-definition, or definition of other. All these are constantly being born, they exist for a while, they change, and then they die. I cannot emphasize this enough. This is perhaps the biggest leap for the mind to make: everything that can be grasped by the mind is subject to birth and death. In this recognition is an opening where, for an instant, there is a true knowing of the permanence of our essential nature. The truth of ourselves has nothing to do with the body, thoughts, emotions, accomplishments, elevated states, or lowered states, which are impermanent.

Who you think you are does not have the capacity to realize the truth of who you are. Truth is too big. Who you think you are appears and disappears in the truth of who you are. Who you truly are can recognize this. You have the right to recognize this. It is nothing that anyone can give you or take away from you. It can be veiled by the powers of mind, but a veil does not really cover anything. When you see a veil, you sense or intuit something behind the veil. What lies behind the veil is the truth of your essential self. The veil is simply your latest self-definition.

Are you willing to recognize that thoughts are simply thoughts, beautiful and horrible in their scope and power, yet inadequate in their description of who you are? Are you willing to investigate this? If so, I invite you to stop thinking, just for a moment. Not as an act of repression, but as a refusal to continue feeding whatever thought arises, to stop building thought upon thought. Whether it is a thought of grandeur or a thought of worthlessness, stop feeding it and recognize it as just a thought.

What can a thought do? It can define experience. It can classify and relegate experience. It can generate experience. But it cannot be experience. A thought has a beginning, a middle, and an end. The absolute truth has no beginning, no middle, and no end. It does not appear and then disappear; it is always here.

I am not against thought. What would be the point of that? Thought is here. Thoughts can be a glorious expression of creativity and understanding—to recognize thought for what it is, is to be neither for nor against it. But when you are free of the bondage of believing that thoughts are *reality,* you are free to enter into the direct experience of who you are. Who you are cannot be captured through thought. The mind cannot capture its source, because the mind is only an aspect of the source, not the whole. You are the source, and since you are the source, you can discover yourself as that.

# THE TRANCE
# OF LANGUAGE    18

L anguage is an incredible power of mind. But if we look at it carefully, we see that it is still in the very primitive stages of development. Everyone can recognize this, just from the experience of trying to communicate with someone else. You know what you said, but they think you said something else. Then there are certain words, like "God," "truth," "eternity," and "self," that put us into a trance based on our past conditioning. When we hear these words, they have a history that deeply influences their meaning.

Perhaps when we first heard the word "God," it was in a very Sunday-schoolish kind of way. Maybe we imagined a big, benevolent father who would take care of us and love us if we were good. Then we grew out of that, but it is still filed away somewhere and still influencing us. God is still a "somebody." At some point maybe God is interpreted as a presence, but that presence is usually thought of as being "somewhere."

The same is true, of course, with the word "truth." "Truth" is heard in the context of the family's truth, the tribe's truth, or the culture's truth, with a particular subconscious meaning in every individual mind.

This most certainly also applies to the word "self." We even get very sophisticated and split that word into higher self and lower self, making the meaning ever more complicated and convoluted. The higher self is the "good" self, which goes to God, and the lower self is the "bad" self, which goes to the devil. This is a primitive and totally conditioned trance. To avoid any confusion, I would like to re-clarify what I mean when I use certain words, because I may not mean what you think I mean.

When I use the word "God," I am not talking about anything that can ever be separate from anything else. The same goes for "truth." I am not speaking of a truth that is subject to change, or personal opinion, or a vote. Truth is changeless. When I use the word "self" or "you," I am speaking to the truth which you are, which cannot be thought, cannot be contained, and cannot be separated into higher or lower, good or bad, because it is not a thing. *You* cannot be contained by any thought, good or bad, superior or inferior, just as God and truth cannot be contained.

# WHERE THE MIND CANNOT GO 19

When we are small children, and we are just beginning to learn how to be people, we get early training on how to get what we want. As infants, we want food more than anything else, and we know instinctively that if we yell, we will get fed. Concurrent with yelling for what we want, we also learn to charm to get what we want, a kind of childish seduction that involves being smart, bright, pretty, good, or even bad.

As we progress, we are sent to school, where we learn reading, writing, and arithmetic. We learn the steps to achieve new goals. These basic steps are the building blocks from which we can learn not only the language of our culture, but also many other languages. We can learn to write not only simple things, but also very elaborate and exquisite expressions of self.

Our learning continues, and we begin to desire broader satisfaction. We choose a career and learn the necessary steps to gain proficiency, and when we're finished with that career, we move on to another one. The techniques and strategies we use to get what we want are very simple at first, becoming increasingly more complex as time goes on.

At some point in a blessed life, there arises the desire for truth. Not just "my" truth, but real truth, final truth, eternal truth. This doesn't happen for everyone. It is a mystery why this desire appears in some people and not in others. The trouble comes, however, when we take our extensive learning techniques and try to apply them to finding truth, and inevitably fail. We may then try to apply other, earlier versions of what seemed to get us what we want, and we fail again.

At this point, when we see that all our sophisticated techniques are useless in fulfilling true spiritual desire, we tend to regress to simple yelling. We may even yell a prayer: "Help me! Take me! Show me!" This prayer is close, but even this doesn't usually work, because we are so absorbed in our yelling that we neglect to see that what we are yelling for is already here. The yelling doesn't work, so we try something else. This is called the cycle of rein- carnation. It is a daily cycle, a monthly cycle, a yearly cycle, a whole lifetime of cycling in and out, in and out, and failing, fail- ing, failing. Yes, there are beautiful glimpses of truth along the way, moments of joy, union, understanding, and wisdom. But the moment these experiences end, we begin yelling again, or searching again, or trying again.

Many people misunderstand what it means to call off the search. It does not mean to give up the desire for truth. It means to stop *searching* for truth, and to stop relying on the mind to orchestrate how truth will be revealed. It means to give up the arrogant belief that you will somehow locate truth and bring it to yourself. This belief is based on the lie that you are separate from truth. When this lie is believed very strongly, it creates further experiences of the lie, until finally you recognize that all the yelling, all the searching, all the figuring out, the gathering of more and more experiences, just leaves you with attention on the search rather than on what is and has always been here.

It is truly a blessed and divine moment in a lifetime when the desire for truth appears. The tragedy is that this desire is often translated into some mental concept of how to get truth, or how to get rid of obstructions to truth. This concept is then worshipped, prayed to, and relied on more than truth itself.

The desire for truth is the longing you feel in your heart. The mental relationship with that longing is all the things you throw at it to try to make it go away because it's bothering you. It won't be satisfied with anything less than pure authenticity, pure being.

If you are willing to stop throwing things at your heart's longing, to stop searching for an escape from the longing, it will reveal its own consummation.

When the mind says, "Go here, do this, try that," you can refuse to listen. You can realize that time after time you have gone here, done this, and tried that without any satisfaction. The invitation now is to stop everything, to simply be still. When you stop all your searching, your justifications, your excuses, what power does thought then have? In a millisecond of stopping, a thought is seen for what it is. In that same millisecond, the presence of truth is recognized.

Yet this habit of searching, of relying on the mind and its latest interpretation of where more truth will be found, is very strong. So the cycling begins once again. Possibly, you have had many experiences of truth, of the eternal presence that the mind cannot conceptualize, and not just while you were on the spiritual search. You've had experiences as a child, as an adult, in nature, in loving relationships, out of the blue, in the middle of a street, or in the middle of the night. You could not have planned these experiences, and yet because of your deep conditioning, you imagine that *you* can do it, that *you* can create truth, that *you* can make God come to you. What a sweet, humbling surprise to find that you can't, and that truth, which is God, is already here.

This is so simple. What you are searching for, you are. I don't mean your body, though the body is no obstruction and is included in you. I don't mean your thoughts or your emotions, your destiny, karma, past, or future, though they are not obstructions either. All of these appear, exist, and disappear in the truth of who you are. You are truth already. *You are consciousness.* Consciousness is spirit. Recognize yourself, and you will see yourself everywhere—in every other human being, in every animal, in every plant, in every rock. Until you recognize yourself, you are still figuring out how to find yourself, how to get more of yourself, how to know what is yourself and what is not yourself.

A very strong habit of the mind is the perceived need to know what will happen if thoughts stop. In the end, you just have to stop and see. You have tried every technique except stopping. If you have not stopped, you are still searching. It is that simple.

# THE MIND'S SURRENDER
## TO SILENCE 20

O ur strongest identification, perhaps even more than the identification with the body, is the identification with the mind. When I use the word "mind," I am refer-ring to certain thoughts, such as "I think I am this body and this person, and therefore this is reality." We give thought the author-ity to define who we are. If I think you are separate from me, based on physical sensations or perceptions, that thought has authority as arbiter of reality.

In our minds, thoughts take the place of God, and they also take the place of the devil. A war is fought between the good thoughts and the bad thoughts. A desire arises to accumulate more good thoughts so that they can defeat the bad thoughts, the forces of light can defeat the forces of darkness. You are conditioned to believe that if the good thoughts win, your higher self wins, and you will be at peace. It is certainly true that the experience of life is enhanced when your mind stream has an abundance of good thoughts. It is equally true that pollution of your mind by negative or bad thoughts results in a poisoned mind and body. Yet what is overlooked is that at the core, there is always peaceful, continuous, unmoving awareness. What you overlook is that who you truly are is already at peace. Winning and losing have nothing to do with the truth of who you are.

Our minds are inactive for many moments during the day, but we are conditioned to pay attention only to the activity of the mind, and these points of silence are simply overlooked. When I speak of "stopping," I am pointing to that silence between thoughts, which is formless consciousness. There is a presence there, and we can recognize that who we are is that presence. We have been taught to believe "I think, therefore I am," rather than the truth, which is "I am, therefore I think."

The trance of conditioned thoughts can be deep and complex, but it has no defense against something as simple as "stop." When you consciously recognize this point of stopping, you have a real choice. Before that recognition, your thoughts are just mechanical actions of the mind based on past conditioning, on desire, or on aversion. After that recognition, you can consciously choose to tell the truth about what is always present before thought, after thought, and during thought. Can *presence* be thought? This question, in effect, crumbles the neat patterns of the mind. It causes a dropping, a release, and relief from the huge illusory world of thought. The balancing and re-balancing and re-forming and re-inventing of what you call "me" is only a thought, with another thought processed on top of that, and then another thought. The moment of recognizing what cannot be thought is the moment of recognizing who you are. It is a moment of the mind's surrender to silence.

I speak a lot about stopping, but perhaps I haven't yet really spoken about it in a way that can be understood. Stopping is, first of all, recognizing that as thoughts arise, you have a choice: your mind can either follow the thoughts or be still, letting them arise without touching them. My invitation to stop is to not build thought upon thought, to not fantasize or replay old events. The choice is for the mind to be still, and in that choice is the possibility of recognizing what is always still, whether there are thoughts or no thoughts.

Stopping first occurs by recognizing the activity of the mind and not following it. Not following mind activity is different from resisting the mind or repressing thoughts. Not following thought has a relaxing, opening quality. Although it may feel unfamiliar, and the fear of the unfamiliar may, in itself, generate mind activity, to stop following thoughts is effortless. In following thoughts and further spinning our stories, the simple and profound ease of being is overlooked.

My invitation in this moment is to do nothing. A thought may appear—do nothing with it. Relax *into* any thought or emotion that arises, and allow the natural ease, the natural truth of who you are, to take precedence over the thought. In this stopping, you can *freshly* recognize the truth of what is always here, the truth of who you are. Now, in this moment, with your mind, choose that truth. Tie your mind to that truth so that whatever challenges may appear, they meet a mind that is tied to the truth, a truth that is confirmed whenever the mind stops.

Stopping is not a practice. It is simply the opportunity to see that within this seemingly endless flow of thoughts, there is a choice to not follow the thoughts. In not following thoughts, the mind stops, and what is here, what is silent, and what is always stopped can be revealed.

In an instant of recognizing the silence that is always here, you recognize your true face. You recognize the presence of God. You realize truth. Then you can address the challenges of life, of bodily pain, emotional turmoil, or mental confusion, with greater clarity and insight, because you no longer identify these states with who you are.

You are existence itself. Existence is consciousness, which is alive, and in love with itself. This theatre of you, me, circumstances, emotions, good events, and bad events is God's theatre. It is not to be avoided, but enjoyed. It is to thrill with, to weep with, but also to recognize, "Oh my God, what a play! What a theatre!"—and in that recognition, to know who you are. You, as consciousness, are the stage upon which the actors move, the screen upon which the film of life is projected, and the animating force present in each actor. Whoever you imagine yourself to be, whatever role you imagine yourself to play, the truth of who you are now is deeper than that role, closer than that role, and also beyond that role. Not who you will be someday, but right now: who you are and have always been.

The ever-present possibility in any moment is to wake up to the truth of yourself as consciousness. That waking up occurs in the mind's surrender to silence.

# SPIRITUAL PRACTICE 21

Many of the people I encounter sincerely want to realize the truth of their being. They ask me, "What do I do? How do I do that?" Paradoxically, this desire for true freedom finally can only be realized if you don't "do" anything to realize it.

There are practices whereby you do mantras, visualizations, prostrations, or some kind of selfless service. They are all designed to still the mind so that it is not obsessing on what is needed to reveal true fulfillment. Practices are excellent for honing the capacity of the mind both to focus and to surrender. Let us acknowledge that our spiritual practices have served us, that they are gifts from masters who have come before us. But let us also recognize that the truth of who we are is here now, and that all our practices have been ways of searching for what is already here, of trying to clear a path back to our own hearts.

The problem is that finally, any attempt to go somewhere implies that you are not already there. In fact, any activity you undertake to achieve this is an obstruction to the deepest recognition of what has always been fully realized.

In this moment, you can realize what does not need to be practiced to exist. This is the easiest, simplest, and most obvious truth. What has kept it a secret throughout the ages is its absolute simplicity and its immediate availability.

This simplicity is difficult, because we are taught from childhood that to achieve something, we have to learn what the steps are and then practice them. This works beautifully for any number of things. The mind is an exquisite learning tool. But self-realization, as well as the deepest inspiration and creativity, come directly from the *source* of the mind. Realization does not come from any doing; it comes from surrendering the mind to the source.

If spiritual practices serve the purpose of stopping the mind, they are strong allies. But if they deepen the belief that you are someone in particular who practices something in particular in order to get something that you do not believe is already here, then they are an obstruction. They keep you spinning around yourself rather than allowing you to deepen into yourself.

Meditation means many different things to different people. It can mean focusing on the breath, or concentrating on an image, or any number of things. But the meditation practice perpetuated by most people in the world is this: "I am this body, I am these thoughts, I am these emotions." There may be breaks where some kind of formal meditation is practiced, but then it's back to the strongest practice: "This is me, I am this body, these are my wants, this is what I have to have, this is what I don't have," and on and on. This is the meditation! And it is a meditation of suffering. Because it is so widespread, it is overlooked. It is thought of not as a practice but as reality.

There are exquisite moments when the usual meditation stops— moments of being absorbed in a lover's embrace, in the sound of beautiful music, or in the colors of a sunrise. There are moments where there is no "you" being practiced; there is simply beingness. And in this simple beingness, there is peace, insight, clarity, and naturalness, an effortless grace and ease of being. But we believe very strongly in our *me* meditation, and so these are usually just brief moments before the normal practice is picked up again: "I am this body; this is who I am. You are that body; that is who you are. This is my culture; that is your culture. These are my beliefs; those are your beliefs. You are my enemy; you are my friend. You want something from me; I want something from you," etc.

I would never discourage anyone from taking breaks from this usual practice of suffering, whether these breaks are found in what is called spiritual practice, or in dancing, listening to music, being in nature, or lying in a hammock. The truth of who you are, however, is simpler than anything that can be practiced. Personal suffering, on the other hand, is very complex, and for it to continue, it must be practiced. If you are suffering, just as an investigation, see if you are *practicing* your suffering.

Since we are so conditioned and attuned to define who we are by particular activities, we spend our lives overlooking the vast ground of stillness that is the simplicity of *being*. When I speak of the "heart," I am speaking of this same *being*. When I speak of the core of every phenomenon, *being* is what I am referring to. When I speak of what is met in self-inquiry, I am also speaking of *being,* whether it is emotional self-inquiry, such as meeting fear, anger, or despair, or mental self-inquiry, such as inquiring into the actual I-thought. To inquire fully into *anything* is to discover this vast, simple presence of *being*—yourself, as you are.

Being is not a practice. A practice involves some technique, a right way and a wrong way, a belief in getting someplace, and a reward or attainment. In the truth of absolute stillness, none of that applies.

By the time I met my teacher, I had attempted many forms of meditation. I had experienced moments of beauty, of transcendence, of true knowing, and yet the underlying longing that accompanied the thoughts, the underlying "How do I get it? How do I keep it? I've got to find a way," was still operating. When I met Papaji, he told me to stop. He extended to me an invitation that I am happy to extend to you. This moment, stop right where you are. Stop all effort to get whatever you *think* will give you fulfillment, whatever you *think* will give you truth. All that is required is one instant of truly stopping.

This one instant is elusive for most people, because as they approach the instant of stopping, an enormous welling of fear usually arises: "If I stop, if I *really* stop, I will slide back and lose the ground that I have gained through my efforts and practices. Even though I am still not fully satisfied, I am more satisfied than I was. I have a better life, my mind is calmer, my circumstances are better, and I might lose all of that."

For me, it was quite extraordinary to hear this "stop." I was certain that he was going to give me some secret knowledge—and he did. But it is only secret because it is so obvious. It is not esoteric. I was certain that he would whisper some magical formula in my ear—and he did. He said, "Stop." It was so simple that I was thrown to the floor. My thoughts stopped, and in that stopping was more fulfillment than could ever be imagined. What we imagine as fulfillment has to do with less pain, less conflict, more pleasure, more peace, more acknowledgement, more love. But true fulfillment cannot be imagined; it can only be realized.

He told me to throw away every strategy, every technique, every tool, and to just be here and receive what he was offering. It soon sank in: "He really means what he says. He is not teaching me a new mantra, or a new practice, or a new set of beliefs, a liturgy, a catechism, or a cosmology. He is not telling me 'what it all means' and 'what will happen' and 'why it came about.'" He was asking me to release all of that from my mind. Not that any of it was wrong. It was just that the hodgepodge of spiritual concepts I had created could never rival unconditional reality.

All the holiest scriptures, texts, and practices come from truth and point back to truth, but there has to be a moment when you leap back into yourself. And that leap happens only right now, when you are naked of everything but yourself, when you are innocent of what you have learned about who you are.

Another question I am often asked is "How do I remain in a state of being 'stopped'?" But stopped is not a state. Neither silence nor stillness is a state. This is a very important distinction. You can get your mind into a state of relative calm, and you can get your body to relax, but the stillness I am referring to is, by its nature, always still. It is always stopped. All mental movement, all doing, appears, exists, and disappears back into this stateless stillness.

A state has a beginning, a middle, and an end. There are happy and sad states, altered and mundane states, high and low states, but the stateless presence of being *is* stillness. Awareness *is* stillness. Who you already are *is* this stillness.

Your mind may be active with thoughts—thoughts about activity or thoughts about trying to stop—but that is all occurring in the statelessness of being, which is stillness itself.

If you can just get it out of your mind that unchanging stillness is something that can be done or practiced, something that you can succeed or fail at doing, then stillness, the presence of being, can finally reveal itself to you as your own self.

Recognize that the impulses to *do* stillness come from the activity of the mind that is appearing in stillness. That stillness is not dead or blank. It is consciousness. It is awareness itself, and you are that awareness. The thoughts, I have to get still, I'm trying to get still, why can't I get still? are being observed by and experienced by stillness itself.

You think yourself to be a thought, and then because you think yourself to be a thought, you think you can lose stillness. Then you think another thought about how to recover what has been lost, and then another thought about your success or failure in that recovery, and then another thought about how great or how horrible you are because you have succeeded or failed. All the while, there is this simple, present stillness that is aware of the whole play. It experiences the play, experiences the suffering of the play, yet is ultimately untouched by the play. The only thing that separates you from recognizing the truth of who you are as eternal stillness is following some thought that says you are not that.

# THE IMPERMANENCE OF
## MENTAL CONSTRUCTS 22

We know how thoughts can dictate the quality of our experience. When we are in love, the world is seen as friendly, bright, and lovely. When we are heartbroken, the world is seen as dark, cold, and menacing. Most people experience their self-worth as fluctuating extremes of positive and negative. The search for more positive experiences, and the avoidance of negative ones, form the common day-to-day strategy of most lives. Unfortunately, if the positive view is clung to and the negative view is run from, the bondage of misidentification continues, and the experience of life remains limited.

This can be hard to accept, because we tend to want to cling to our beautiful states of mind, to happy sensations and wonderful moments. If they could be successfully clung to, then what would be the harm? But all beautiful states of mind are inherently impermanent, so they cannot be successfully clung to. All states of mind and all feelings arise, exist, and then disappear. Most people spend most of their day avoiding this truth through thought activity. That thought activity is primarily motivated by the desire to get back wonderful feelings from the past, and to get rid of any bad feelings that may arise in the present.

When you see clearly the relentless, ruthless truth of the impermanence of bodies, emotions, thoughts, states, and images, you will have the choice to let what is impermanent be impermanent. What an easy choice! It is already impermanent. In fact, all of the activity to hold onto what is inherently impermanent is finally recognized as futile. In your willingness to accept the truth of impermanence, which includes every idea of who you are, there is the deepest relaxation.

Your idea of who you are when you are five is different from your idea of who you are when you are fifteen, fifty, or ninety. An idea, by its nature, is impermanent. Recognize that any idea of who you are is impermanent. Anything that is impermanent has no inherent reality. In this complete recognition, all activity of the mind is stopped.

Mind activity feeds on itself until it creates an enormous complexity of suffering. At the core of all mind activity is a search for self-definition, but the mind searches in all the wrong places. It searches in thoughts. It searches in objects—acquiring a new car, a

new lover, a better job, a bigger house. It even searches in spirituality, in the quest for the enlightened "me."

The mind's activity is always based on rejecting something or
grasping at something. Whatever the mind is rejecting or clinging to
is impermanent. When your mind surrenders to the truth of impermanence, this activity has nowhere to go, and the mind is still. At
this point, the mind has reached the ocean of consciousness, realizing itself as never separate from that ocean. The *permanence* of your
true nature is recognized to be the continuous presence of awareness
that was exactly the same when you were five, fifteen, fifty, or ninety
years old. Subtle, radiant awareness is your true identity. When you
realize who you are, and all your attempts to get something better
so that you can be something better are seen in all their absurdity, a
great, deep laugh follows. Such a release, this laugh. It comes from
millions of aeons of hiding from the truth of yourself, and then the
exquisite release of finally surrendering to the truth of being.

## MEMORY AND PROJECTION 23

T he only obstacle to realizing the truth of who you are is *thinking* who you are. It is really that simple. I use all of my conversations with people to cut through that thought process, which as you know is very strong. The thoughts of who you are come from two powers of mind: the power of remembering the past and the power of projecting into the future. Thoughts of past and future create the present thought of who you are.

These powers of memory and projection are very big powers indeed. There is nothing wrong with remembering the past or projecting into the future. Both are part of the experience and the power of being human. However, the danger of this power is that in overlooking permanent presence, in being so fascinated by God's fabrications and the permutations of those fabrications,

God Itself is overlooked. Then suffering appears, and a yearning arises to reconnect with the truth of God to alleviate the suffering.

Right now, before you read any further, I want you to close your eyes and generate some thoughts. Everyone is a master at this, so you might as well use it. See yourself as a child; see who you were then. You may have a picture, or a sensation, or just a sense of knowing who you were then. Now see yourself as an adolescent or young adult. See who you were then.

See yourself as you are when you are sick, when you feel miserable. Experience the feelings and the thoughts of being sick. Now see yourself when you are bursting with health. See who you are then. Feel the sensations that arise around the image of yourself as the healthy one.

See yourself happy, really fulfilled, and imagine how that feels. Now see yourself as miserable, lost, isolated, and separate.

See yourself as who you imagine you will be someday. Project yourself into the future.

Now, most important, see if it is possible to tell the truth: What is it that sees all these images of you? What is it that is aware of all your feelings? The notions of who you are have an age, they change, they appear in the past, and they are projected into the future. What sees these changes has always been here, changelessly seeing. The seeing does not have a face, does not have a personality, and finally, does not even have an essence. It is without thought, without attribute, without past, and without future. And yet, when there are attributes, a past, a future, it is not absent. It is eternally here.

If you were able, in that split second, to see the emptiness of any image of who you are, then you can choose to either continue chasing some better image, or surrender to the truth that is both imageless and inseparable from any image. This is very important. The formless truth of who you are is inseparable from any formulation of who you are, for it is all-inclusive.

Right now, in this present moment, the formless truth of who you are is just as present as when your body is dead and all those images are finished. Your incredible and thrilling opportunity is to realize yourself as the formless truth before your body dies.

Many of you have realized this. Many of you will realize this. Some may not realize it until they are on their deathbed. Even in that moment of death, if you can realize the formless presence that has been inseparable from every moment of your life, then your life will have been lived in the glory of that conscious awareness. Your final fulfillment will be a testimony to the world.

The thoughts of yourself are the only obstacle to this fulfillment, yet they are not a problem because you, as consciousness, have the capacity to see through any obstacle. You are the seeing itself. You have full and absolute capacity to know yourself, to be true to yourself, and to be tested in this knowing. In that testing, you will discover and know yourself in ways that are deeper and always fresher.

# COMPARISON AND POSESSION 24

Another power of the mind is the power to go through experience and sort it, putting it into the correct categories. What can be seen, sorted, and categorized is within the realm of the mind. Some things are ugly, some are beautiful, some are good, some are bad, but who you are is none of that. Who you are cannot be seen. It can be directly experienced, however, and it is always being experienced.

Because of our infatuation with the sorting capacity of the mind, we overlook this ongoing experience of what cannot be seen and what is absolutely the same in everyone, regardless of gender, race, culture, class, nervous system, intellect, or sophistication. It is closer than any concept of enlightenment or any concept of ignorance.

If you will, for one moment, stop feeding the tendency of the mind to compare and to polarize, what a laugh appears. What a laugh! "I had hair and I was trying to be bald. I had brown eyes and I thought blue would do it. I was Western and I thought I should be Eastern. I was female and I thought I needed to be male." Those are just gross examples. It gets very, very subtle. In the mind's practice of sorting, comparing, and polarizing, there is a tragic overlooking of the sameness of one self. The *main* focus of the mind's power is to possess. Learning takes place by possessing knowledge in the mind. Learning is an awesome and wondrous power, which requires the possessing function of the mind. This power facilitates the great arts, the great scientific discoveries, and the capacity to design and build a house, a piece of clothing, or a meal. But where the mind cannot go, what it cannot possess, is the source of its own power.

Once the attention of an individual lifetime is turned mysteriously and sacredly toward its own source, toward reunion with God, the realm of the mind is of no use. Because we are so in love with the power of our minds, it may take lifetimes to discover this truth. We don't want to believe that there is somewhere our minds cannot go. We don't want to even consider that in order to realize the absolute truth of our existence, we may have to let go of everything.

We cannot possess truth; that would be the mind's idea. But truth can claim its possession, which is *us,* each soul, each being.

When I speak of "stopping" or "calling off the search," I am simply pointing to our habitual tendency to try to get something, which we have been trained to do with the facilities of our minds, through powers of thinking, projecting, imagining, discriminating, or veiling. But just in one instant of simply being—without being anybody, without being anything, without getting it right, without missing it, without naming it, and without knowing it—awakening is present. The truth is that everyone has these moments every day, but they are overlooked because of our infatuation with the powers of the mind. The mind is not present in any of these pure and perfect moments. But then the mind arises again, and we get on with our business, with our definitions, and with our ideas of who has wronged us, what we need, or what we have to know.

To realize true freedom, this infatuation with the mind must be cut, and to be cut, it must first be seen. Each of us needs to investigate and then tell the truth. In telling the truth, the mind is used to expose and bust itself. In lying, the mind stays in power. When the mind is busted, a deep happiness is revealed. Then the intellectual and creative capacities of every individual, the life experiences of every individual, can all be joyfully used in service to the truth.

The invitation to discover love, truth, enlightenment, freedom, or yourself carries with it the ruthless fact that the mind cannot deliver it. All that is truly pure and free is unknowable. That is the humbling of the mind. That is the essential understanding that the mind *can* comprehend. That is the mental doorway to surrender.

Because you have had success in knowing many things, you hope that if you just work hard enough, you will succeed. But the realization of true freedom is the opposite of working hard mentally. The perseverance you need here is to give up the hope that the mind can deliver freedom; give up the hope that the mind can deliver the heart, which is love; give up the hope that the mind can deliver enlightenment, which is truth. In that recognition, surrender can naturally follow.

# STRATEGIES OF
# THE SUPEREGO 25

The ego and its partner, the superego, are internal mental voices that appear to determine who you are. As the "I am this body" thought (ego) determines your individual reality, the thoughts that determine how your ego is doing, how it could be better, or why it never will be better, as well as how others are doing, are the voices of your superego. Your ego is a simulation, a virtual reality of "I am," based on perception, sense experiences, and learning. Your superego is a simulation of authority designed to control your ego. It is based on feedback from others in your life.

Both ego and its further development, superego, are wondrous phenomena. There is nothing inherently wrong with them. Both have an extraordinary role to play in the theatre of human consciousness. The development of ego is miraculous and the formation of superego is perhaps even more astonishing. The problem arises when they command most of your attention and life force. Your opportunity to spontaneously and authentically experience life is then preempted by attention to the internal war: the voices that state, "I am this or that," versus the counterpoint, "You are not enough of this or that." Some voices say you are good, beautiful, and kind, while other voices say you are horrible, ugly, and miserable.

A simple example: If you bang your head accidentally, after the initial shock and sensation of pain, what mental voices do you hear? Do they deal with blame? If so, do they blame you or someone else or some object? These voices arise from your superego's attempt to assert control, usually through verbal punishment, so that head banging won't happen again. The superego is your internalized authority, where part of your ego splits off and calls itself "God" or "Mother" or "Father" or "Guru." When you recognize this split, a great inner battle is exposed, especially in the "spiritual" arena where the superego desires to get rid of the ego. Only the superego wants to get rid of the ego. Getting rid of the ego is the ultimate control. Only your superego needs war. These warring thoughts are, of course, reflected in our collective world as well as in our individual world. However, for our purposes here, put your attention on what is going on in your egoic reality, not because it should or shouldn't be happening, but simply to discover what is being thought of as real.

We can cherish the freedoms granted by family, culture, and government, but they are ultimately meaningless if we are bound internally by a simulation of authority. Reliance on superego is buttressed by our fear of what we would be without it. In short, we generally have a deeply embedded distrust of our core self. We actually distrust the freedom we crave.

The question is, can you recognize a mistake (banging your head) and can you know what is wrong (acts requiring moral choices of conscience) without a punishing or rewarding fabricated authority? Regardless of the appropriate functions of ego/superego in the past, in this moment are you willing to trust what you have learned? And even more radically, are you willing to trust the integrity at the core? If there is an *ambition* to be egoless, it is a red flag. What is wrong with the ego? Who has a problem with the ego? Does awareness have a problem with the ego? Only the superego has a problem with the ego, and it is a huge problem. The superego wants to control the ego.

In recognizing the tendency of the superego to dominate the ego, without then having to establish a *super*-superego, you can simply welcome ego with its ambition and needs. In this moment, you can welcome them all—ego, superego, internal and external illusion—into the limitless consciousness that you truly are. Then you can experience yourself as a very limited human being with limited propensities.

Another very common battering ram of the superego is the idea of "worthlessness," especially in spiritual circles where there tends to be a great fear of arrogance. But arrogance and worthlessness are just two sides of the same coin of ego. Neither experience needs to be avoided. Both can simply be met and directly investigated. If you just allow yourself to be *fully and completely* arrogant for one second, you will see the absurdity of arrogance, its posturing, its emptiness. It is exactly the same with worthlessness. If you fully and completely experience one second of true, absolute worthlessness, worthlessness will become nothing. It will reveal itself to be just another weapon of the superego, having nothing to do with the truth of who you are. Whether you run from arrogance, worthlessness, or *any* experience, you are constricting the life force. You are desperately attempting to be what you think you should be, while being haunted by what you think you are.

Another interesting twist in the recognition of the superego is that if the superego is engaged in battle with the ego, it will definitely win. It is designed to win because it has "God" on its side. It is the authority. Whatever measly little arguments the ego can throw up, the superego will win, case closed. The impulse to listen to and be beaten by the superego is huge, but the willingness to stop and see what is under it will reveal the reality of the spaciousness beyond all faces of the superego. Then you will see that the superego is just sound and fury, signifying nothing but conditioned learning. But because this is the way that we as human animals are taught by our parents, cultures, and religions, their voices are very deeply ingrained.

The core strategy of the superego is the system of rewards and punishments. It's pretty primitive, but it works. You must see how you speak to yourself internally, and how you speak to others in terms of reward or punishment. Otherwise, this thought-form called "superego," which says "I am the authority, I know what is right and what is wrong," continues to operate subconsciously.

There is nothing wrong with rewards and punishments. They are very effective learning devices. They may be appropriate in terms of how you train children, pets, students, or co-workers. They may work in any number of arenas. But when you are dealing with the desire and longing for truth, then the strategies of reward and punishment are distractions of the mind. The mind is still assuming control as "truth giver" or "truth judge." But truth is out of the realm of the mind. It is uncontrollably free. It cannot be punished or rewarded.

As a way of investigating how the superego operates within your own mind, you can once again inquire directly within, letting the answers float freely up from the subconscious. Ask yourself these two questions: *How do I punish?* and *How do I reward?*

Make no distinction between internal or external punishment or reward.

When you determine that you have done something well, what praise do you give yourself? Special treats? Tender words of love? And if you determine that you have done poorly, what punishment: Harsh words? Anger? Hate?

At first your answers may seem to be obvious, things that you already know. But then perhaps you will be surprised, and that is really the point of self-inquiry: to be open enough to discover what you were previously unaware of, that was unknown and unexamined—in this case, to discover how the superego manifests itself within your own mind. Whether the answers are spiritual or worldly, enlightened or mundane, is totally irrelevant.

See, feel, and experience in your mind what is revealed in this inquiry. Maybe you have many more rewarding strategies than punishing strategies. Maybe they equal each other. Maybe you are punishing yourself now for punishing yourself before. The key is the willingness to see the workings of your own mind without making them right or wrong, without adding to the power to strategize. See if there is an inner burning that can occur in the exposure of the strategies. If there is a burning and it is not avoided but surrendered to, what does it reveal?

When the mind begins to reactivate, take another moment to let all strategies go, to discover what is underneath it all, before it all, after it all, what is always here, what cannot be revoked, and what cannot be awarded.

# DIRECTLY EXPERIENCING THE EMOTIONS 26

The questions I am most frequently asked are related to the emotions. Many people seek to be free from difficult emotions such as anger, fear, and grief, and seek the more pleasant emotions such as joy, happiness, and bliss. The usual strategies for achieving happiness involve either repressing or expressing negative emotions in the hope that they will be pushed from sight or released. Unfortunately, neither way reflects the truth of one's inherent self, which is an unmoving purity of being that exists deeper than any emotion and remains unaffected by any emotion.

There are certainly times when it is appropriate to repress or express an emotion. But there is also another possibility: to neither repress nor express. I call this "direct experience."

To directly experience any emotion is to neither deny it nor wallow in it, and this means that there can be no *story* about it. There can be no storyline about who it is happening to, why it is happening, why it should not be happening, who is responsible, or who is to blame.

In the midst of any emotion, so-called "negative" or "positive," it is possible to discover what is at the core. The truth is that when you really experience any negative emotion, it disappears. And when you truly experience any positive emotion, it grows and is endless. So *relatively*, there are negative and positive emotions, but in inquiry, only positive ones: that is the positivity that is absolute consciousness. Because there is not much in our culture that confirms this astounding revelation, we spend our lives chasing positive emotions and running from negative emotions.

When you fully experience any negative emotion, with no story, it instantaneously ceases to be. If you think you are fully experiencing an emotion and it remains quite intense, then recognize that there is still some story being told about it—how big it is, how you will never be able to get rid of it, how it will always come back, how dangerous it is to experience it. Whatever the story of the moment may be, the possibilities of postponing direct experience are endless.

For instance, when you are irritated, the usual tendency is to do something to get rid of the irritation or to place blame on either yourself or someone or something else as the cause of the irritation.

Then the storylines around irritation begin to develop. It is actually possible to do nothing with the irritation, to not push it out of awareness or try to get rid of it, but to directly experience it. In the moment that irritation arises, it is possible to simply be completely, totally, and freely irritated, without expressing it or repressing it.

In general, direct experience often reveals a deeper emotion. Irritation is perhaps just a ripple on the surface. Deeper than irritation, there may actually be rage or fear. Again, the goal is neither to get rid of the rage or the fear, nor to analyze it, but to directly experience it. If rage or fear is revealed to be beneath irritation, then let your awareness go deeper; let yourself be absolutely, completely angry or fearful, without acting out or repressing.

Fear is often the biggest challenge, because it is what most people habitually attempt to keep away. Of course, as they try to keep it away, it grows even larger, hovers even closer.

What I am suggesting is that you can actually open to fear; you can experience being afraid without any need to say you are afraid, and without following any thought of being afraid. You can just simply experience fear itself.

When I speak of directly experiencing fear, I am not speaking about physiologically appropriate fear. The response to physical danger, fight or flight, is natural and appropriate to the human organism. It is hardwired into the body for its survival. For instance, it is appropriate to get out of the way of an approaching bus. But the fears that I suggest be directly met, all the way through, are the psychological fears, the fears that keep our energy and attention bound unnecessarily in protection and defense, such as the fear of emotional pain or the fear of loss or death. When a psychological fear is met rather than resisted and run from, it often reveals an even deeper emotion.

A deep sadness or hurt may be revealed under fear. This, too, can be directly and completely experienced with no need of a storyline. If you are willing to experience these emotional layers all the way through, you will finally approach what appears to be a deep abyss. This abyss is what the mind perceives as nothingness, emptiness, no-body-ness. This is an important moment, because the willingness to be absolutely nothing, to be nobody, is the willingness to be free. All these other emotional states are layers of defense against this experience of nothingness—the death of who you think you are. Once the defenses are down, once the door is open, then this nothingness that has been feared can be met fully. This meeting is the revelation of true self-inquiry, revealing the secret gem of truth that has been hidden in the core of your own heart all along. The diamond discovered *is you*.

This is an immense discovery, but you have to discover it for yourself. If you are willing to deeply, completely experience any emotional state, you will discover at its core the same pristine awareness meeting itself as both the experiencer and the experienced. If you can discover this truth first hand, you will be freed from running away from so-called negative states and running toward so-called positive ones. You will be freed from either rejecting or clinging to what is inherently impermanent. You will be freed to truly meet yourself and rejoice in this meeting.

Whatever emotion arises in consciousness can be fully met by consciousness, with no need to hide in stories or analysis. In your willingness to not follow the workings of the mind, but to just be still and completely experience whatever emotion is arising, you will see that it is nothing. Emotions are only held together by thought, whether that thought is conscious or subconscious.

You have the power to simply stop and say, "Fear, anger, grief, despair—okay, come." When you say, "Okay, come," and you really mean it, and you are truly open, the emotion cannot come, because in that moment, you are not telling a story about it. I invite you to check this out for yourself. Fear, anger, grief, or despair only exists when linked to a story! Yes, this is an amazing, simple, yet profound discovery. It is huge! You can actually recognize that what you are running away from does not, in truth, finally exist, and what you are running toward is already always here.

When Columbus and other explorers discovered the "New World," they all came back and said, "There is more out there than we know about. The earth is not flat." But many people responded, "Oh no, I am not going there. The sea demons will get me. I will fall off the earth." It is with this same primitivism that we view our emotions. If you are willing to fall off the edge of the earth, you will see that you yourself hold the earth, and you cannot "fall off" from yourself; you can only go deeper into yourself.

On the opposite end of the spectrum, in the Western spiritual subculture, in particular, people are fairly open to experiencing their emotions, because it gives them a sense of depth and a sense of freedom. But this can become a cover for the fear of experiencing no emotion whatsoever. Defining yourself as an emotional being is perhaps a step deeper than defining yourself as a purely mental being, but it is not all the way home. What you avoid in defining yourself as an emotional being is emotion-less-ness, nothingness, emptiness. Once you have experienced pure emptiness, you know directly that who you are cannot be defined by any mental or emotional state, and this knowledge is freedom.

When you do not define yourself by emotional states, then the emotions are free to arise because they don't mean anything about who you are. You know directly that all states are simply passing through the pure space that is your true nature.

I invite you all the way in to the heart of pure being, not to get rid of any emotion, not to dramatize or glorify any emotion, but to discover what every emotion is calling for, to die to who you think you are before who you think you are dies.

# PART THREE

---

## UNRAVELING
## THE KNOT OF
## SUFFERING

# THE ROOTS OF
## SUFFERING  27

Ignorance is the root of suffering. When I use the word "ignorance," I am speaking about ignoring the truth of who you are in favor of some problem or identification with suffering. Ignoring the limitless truth of yourself, ignoring the eternal presence of divinity, of beingness itself, is the very source of conditioned suffering. Conditioned suffering occurs when your concepts of happiness, truth, and freedom are seen as separate from who you already are.

When I speak of suffering, I am not speaking of the compassionate suffering experienced when one witnesses the anguish in the world. In the acknowledgement of that anguish, suffering can be experienced. This is part of the texture of life, and it is appropriate. Suffering may even be a necessary part of life. By conditioned suffering, I am referring to what could be called "unnecessary" suffering, when you are wrapped up in replaying your own or the world's dramatic stories over and over in your mind.

Unnecessary suffering is actually the *resistance* to suffering. Unnecessary suffering can be dropped in an instant, yet it is usually perpetuated through cycles of mental and emotional activity as an attempt to escape the experience of emotional pain.

Horror and tragedy are happening throughout the globe right now. Certainly, we are aware of the horror and suffering in Africa, in the streets of our cities, within our own families, our own homes, and our own psyches. To be finished with suffering does not mean to ignore suffering. To be true to the eternal truth of who you are is not to ignore anything. What you are finished with is your *fixation* on suffering. This does not mean adopting a substitute fixation on some *idea* of enlightenment or heaven or nirvana. It means recognizing that you have the capacity to realize yourself as not separate from the totality of life. The degree to which you are willing to stop ignoring is the degree to which you are willing to truly know yourself.

People often begin the spiritual life as an escape from the miseries of their worldly life. This is legitimate. It is the way we begin, but it is not the way we end. The ending, which is surrender, is the recognition that no escape is possible or needed. This means fully embracing whatever appears in consciousness rather than ignoring any of it. This embrace is not passive acceptance, or resignation, but the deep meeting of consciousness (subject) with an appearance in consciousness (object). The embrace of consciousness (subject) with an appearance in consciousness (object) reveals total consciousness. When consciousness meets itself in "other," then the conditioned beliefs that you are different from anyone else, that you are less than or greater than anyone else, lose their power. Regardless of your tribe, nation, or spiritual conviction, these distinctions are finished as reality. The story of "difference" is revealed to be an imagined story.

Many of us live privileged and precious lives. You may even recognize the preciousness of your life. But your recognition is useless if you don't recognize that the privilege of your life is not an escape from what is happening in the Middle East or in any ghetto. It is all one *self.* The willingness to be true to who you are is the willingness to see yourself everywhere.

People have asked me if, after spiritual awakening, it still matters that there is hatred, genocide, and continuing violence in the world. Yes, it matters. It matters because it is all a reflection of our own minds. There is nothing going on in the world that is not going on in our own minds. In your willingness to see the truth of that, to experience the horror of that, and finally to see what is also forever untouched by that, you are at least one aspect of consciousness that knows itself to be free. In that *living* knowledge, which ignores nothing, it is possible to make yourself useful to all of life.

# THE DEFINITION
## OF SUFFERING  28

B oth the particulars and the whole of all personal suffering stem from overlooking the truth of who you are in favor of the story of who you are, which is ego. To a two-year-old who is just beginning to sense his or her individualism, that story can start out as very pleasurable or grandiose, inviting the mind to follow it and build on it. Invariably, in the belief that you are limited to being a character in a story, there will be suffering. It is a lie. You are not just a character in a story. You are the totality of being.

The belief that you are just a character in a story, or perhaps even the main character, takes a tremendous amount of maintenance. It takes holding on to the pleasurable aspects of the story, and then attempting to keep out anything that would destroy that "good" story. Then there are the attempts to blame others who don't agree with the story or don't somehow validate or contribute to the story of your worth.

Eventually, a kind of exhaustion sets in. Finally, the ego deflates when something physical, mental, or emotional happens that causes the story to crash. The mind then begins developing its powers of projection, and a search ensues to get out of the deflated state and to find some way into a better version of itself. What follows this search for inflation is the roller coaster of emotions: the roller coaster of "I am great, I am horrible, I am beautiful, I am ugly. The universe gives me what I want; the universe withholds from me." Almost anyone can relate to this. As long as there is hope that the roller coaster of "I am great, I am horrible," will stabilize, this hope is pinned on the character in the story being stable. There actually is no hope for the character in the story to stabilize, as it is continually manipulated by ever-larger external and internal events. Equanimity or stabilization, however, is already present in the truth. Truth holds the story. It is not separate from the story. It permeates both the character and the story.

The huge suffering of personal identification is centered around what does not even exist. The story of who you are does not actually exist. Personal identification begins with a thought, a thought that gathers power because it is bowed to and practiced daily. Then other thoughts are collected to support it, to augment it, and to attempt to perfect it. Who you are thought to be is imagined, fabricated from a string of thoughts, a mind-generated character. When who you are thought to be is examined fully, it is discovered to be nothing.

Personal identification has to do with a "me," a body, an ego, getting what it wants. Maybe the body wants more food, more shelter, or more clothing. Maybe the ego wants more power, more status, more recognition, more enlightenment. Anyone can look in their life and see how this drive for more, if it is out of balance, can keep them from recognizing the perfect joy and fulfillment of simply existing. Even without ever having more of anything, if this moment is fully met, *in this moment* there is more than enough of the bliss of being. But as long as there is an attachment to the story of an individual who needs to get more and keep more, the absolute fulfillment that is always present as the truth of our being will be overlooked.

# THE DIFFERENCE BETWEEN PAIN AND SUFFERING

## 29

I am sometimes asked about the difference between pain and suffering. Pain is sensation in the body at a particular time. Suffering is spread over time and must be accompanied by some story about the pain. The story can, of course, have infinite strands and arrangements—who caused the pain, why, when, how, the metaphysics of it—but the particulars of the story only serve as a distraction and as resistance to the pain itself.

Most people aren't willing to give up their investment in mental and emotional suffering. In the willingness to stop the suffering, which means to stop the *story* about the pain, the pain can be experienced just as it is. What has been previously thought of as unbearable can be experienced with an open mind, because the mind is no longer closed around some idea about the experience. The mind is open. It has dropped all definitions. When pain is met with an open mind, then pain, like every phenomenon, reveals the truth at its core.

Suffering is the mental, emotional, and physical contraction around pain, the history, justification, blame, sentimentalizing, and dramatization of the pain. In the willingness to simply and directly experience any kind of pain, just for an instant, you will discover that the essence of pain is intelligence, clarity, joy, peace—the same essence as bliss! The truth of yourself is revealed even in the midst of pain, and pain is revealed to be another vehicle for truth. In following the story of the pain, this vehicle is overlooked, and the potential gift of pain is wasted.

Let me emphasize that wishing to alleviate pain is natural and appropriate. Medications, the embrace of a loved one, communion with nature, the rhapsody of music and art, are all used to alleviate pain. None of these is a problem. The problem is that the choice of meeting the pain, of stopping the resistance to pain, goes unrecognized. That you have the freedom to stop and intimately face what is tormenting you, at any level, is generally unknown. The lack of recognition for such a choice keeps you bound as the victim of some tormentor. The surprise that awaits this choice is the discovery of what is alive and waiting in the heart of *everything*—spacious consciousness, love, that which heals all, even death.

Who can say what pain will come into your life? Certainly all of us have experienced pain of one kind or another. If you have had the experience of surrendering in the moment that pain arises, of actually opening your mind to pain, whether it is physical, emotional, personal, or worldly, then you have discovered a secret wisdom. In this discovery, you are no longer preoccupied with personal pain, and then there is one less whining, screaming, crying, "What about me?" What a relief! This "one less" is huge, because when the story of personal pain no longer has prominence, you can experience pain you had no idea existed—your neighbor's pain, your parents' pain, your children's pain, the pain of the universe— and in that, you are not making war with what is painful, or hiding from potential future pain. You are living a life open to meet what is here. Then pain, as any experience, is to be bowed to as none other than truth itself.

# SUFFERING IS NOT THE PROBLEM    30

Although it may sound surprising, I do not intend to help anyone get rid of their suffering. Suffering is not the problem. Rather than trying to get rid of suffering, it is more important to inquire into the suffering itself, to investigate the reality of the sufferer. Inquiry is the front door.

The inquiring mind is an open mind, willing to explore most deeply. In that openness, it can allow the presence of suffering without rejecting it or trying to escape it. This can be just as powerful, just as terrifying, and just as profound as facing your own death. When you inquire into suffering, you *meet* suffering, and when you meet suffering, it is possible to discover that suffering is not what you thought it was. In a direct meeting between subject and object, sufferer and suffering, both disappear. Both are discovered, in reality, to be nonexistent.

I will make an even more precise and outrageous statement. I recommend that you consciously suffer. What is wrong with suffering? What thought or voice in your head says suffering is wrong? Painful, yes, but not wrong.

Willingness to suffer fully, even for an instant, without trying to escape or be saved, means that suffering is no longer an obstacle to full surrender into the mystery of existence. Relief from suffering stops being the goal.

According to the Gospel of Thomas, Jesus said, "When you know how to suffer, you do not suffer." The "how to" of suffering is to suffer *all the way*. It is to suffer with full consciousness. To consciously suffer is to consciously recognize the impulse to escape and instead face directly whatever is appearing, be it grief, horror, extreme loss, or sadness.

Suffering is a huge temptress that would have you believe you are not whole, and the recurrence of suffering time and time again becomes the superego's proof that you are not whole.

See if any of your mental, physical, or emotional energy is bound up in resistance to suffering. If you can tell the truth about that without analyzing it, you will recognize in an instant that you have the choice to drop every defense and actually meet the suffering. What is revealed is very good news, but it can only truly be known as good news when you discover it yourself. And it can only truly be discovered when it is discovered for the first time, each time. Otherwise, inquiry becomes just another technique of the mind to avoid suffering.

If you find that self-inquiry becomes just another subtle technique to build a barrier against suffering, then it is important, first of all, to tell the truth about that, and secondly, to broaden your notion of what true self-inquiry is.

When you meet suffering head-on, you make the exquisite, paradoxical discovery that suffering holds the very jewel that was sought in the attempt to escape it. Whether the particular suffering is individual, national, or planetary, that jewel is here now.

Whatever action may or may not follow that meeting is irrelevant. If you are a social activist, a health professional, a hospice worker, a parent, or any other person who works to help alleviate suffering, you will be better at your work when you yourself have met fully what your clients and patients are struggling with.

Meeting suffering has to do with the willingness to be absolutely still, to tell the truth regardless of the intensity of the experience. In the core of suffering is revealed the jewel of what is real, what is true, who you are.

## SEE WHAT CAUSES YOUR SUFFERING 31

The unwillingness to actually see what causes your suffering is what keeps your mind bound in cycles of suffering.

Are you willing to see what causes your suffering? If so, then you are willing for everything to change. *Everything.* Yes, it is a radical notion. This is where most people start backing away.

Finally, when the body dies, your personal story as you experience it will be finished. But you can let the story be finished right now. Lose the whole story. Lose it all. Lose what is great and what is horrible. This loss reveals true freedom.

In your willingness to see what causes your suffering, perhaps you will recognize that you don't even know the causes. To be willing to see what the suffering is really about opens up the possibility of your entire life changing. This is when most people start closing their minds, because they don't want to lose some wonderful aspects of their lives. Most everyone only wants to lose suffering. Until there is a willingness to lose everything to see what causes your suffering, it is impossible to follow what is calling you home.

I can remember reading the wisdom of great teachers and great scriptures. I would nod with the teaching and say, "Yes, I know that is true, I feel that is true." Then I would leave the room and go right back into my particular neurotic infatuation with suffering. I was seeking happiness, of course, in my own particular way. But most important, I was still trying to get rid of my suffering rather than really being truthful about the cause of it.

You have the opportunity in this moment to inquire into yourself, to tell the truth to yourself: *Am I suffering? Where is the suffering? What is it?* If you are telling yourself some story about how it is unenlightened to suffer, then you are keeping that story of suffering conveniently out of sight and out of mind, perpetuating itself in your subconscious and then getting projected onto others. Then your mother, your lover, your teacher, the government, or God is to blame for your misery. Obviously, your relationships can cause tremendous pain, and many relationships must be altered or ended to stop the cycle of pain. But now, for this moment, you can put aside the story of the causes of your suffering, and simply meet whatever you believe to be the source of your suffering. Again, it is the dissolution of the subject and the object, of "you" and "other." It is the inquiry into what is here now.

To invite a meeting with suffering, it may be helpful to imagine a painful relationship or event from your past. Recognize any movement of your mind toward avoidance. Let those thoughts drop away and meet the suffering directly.

In this moment, can you find a sufferer? Are you aware of a discrete entity, or are you perhaps aware of a vast empty space filled with intelligence that is conscious of itself? What is the boundary between who you are and this space? Where is the suffering now? Can you see that this moment of true meeting is not separate from *every* moment of your life?

# HEALING THE PRIMAL WOUND 32

When you desire freedom, then you have to be willing to face what you have been running from in your search for it. In general, most people are running from some kind of pain, usually an infantile one resulting from needs that were not met in childhood. The pain may have both physical and psychological components. It may have a story attached to it, or it may just be an energy field, such as a sense of negativity or dread.

Multiple wounds are part of every life, even among the most privileged. Unless you are successful at dissociating, the whole of human woundedness is somehow present in you. Some people are successful at creating scar tissue over their psyches, over their emotional and physical wounds, and then just getting on with daily life. But I suspect no one is entirely successful, and this failure is a good thing, because then the wound calls attention to itself just as grit in your shoe won't let you be comfortable until you actually attend to it.

Of course, we search in multiple ways, both spiritual and worldly, to make that core ache go away. The thrust of most of the mind's activity is to escape this essential, primal hurt and all the peripherals of that hurt. Perhaps at some point, we even turn to the spiritual life with the hope that a particular teaching or enlightenment will take our wounds away. We try to do what the teaching or the teacher says, and we do it over and over in the hopes that the suffering will leave us.

Surprisingly, a true teacher and a true teaching will throw you, with the greatest compassion and ruthlessness, directly into the center of the wound itself.

The deepest, most essential wound doesn't even have a name. You can call it "the human condition," or "conditioned existence," or "the fact of suffering," and there is a huge drive to escape it, even though it is actually that very drive that eventually brings you full circle to meet the wound. Maturity evolves after you have tried the numerous avenues of escape, only to find that same woundedness still waiting for you.

Many of us have attempted to heal our wounds through psycho-therapy, and psychological work can be very useful. Western culture, in particular, is a psychological culture. Psychological work can be useful in that it fosters a mental maturity where particular patterns and habitual responses can be seen. But psychological work can take you only so far. While it can generate insights that are amazing and humbling, it doesn't really touch the true ground of suffering. It may lead you to the recognition that even with all of your psychological or mental insight, the ground of suffering still remains, and in this way, it serves enormously. It is at this point that you can ask yourself the question, *Well, then, what* will *remove this ground of suffering?* Even if you have worked on yourself psychologically for twenty, forty, or fifty years, if the ground of suffering is still in place, there is something essential that is yet to be revealed.

Healing wounds is appropriate. There is treatment for all wounds, and wounds that can be tended are to be tended. The problem only arises when truth itself is sought through healing. While the emotional, physical, or mental wounding is addressed, that which, by its nature, is whole, pure, free, and at peace goes overlooked. Truth is already here, regardless of the state of your body, your emotions, your mind, or your circumstances.

I invite you, for just this moment, to stop searching for relief from suffering. The invitation is neither to become oblivious to suffering nor to give up in despair. It is an invitation to stop searching for something to rescue you from yourself.

When I met Papaji, and he told me to "stop," I could hear the many reasons in my mind not to stop. First of all, who was *he*, telling me to stop? What if he took over my mind? What if something bad happened to me? It's not safe to stop. Rather, it is safe to think, to figure it out, to go for what is safe, and to avoid what is unsafe.

Practical safety has its place, of course, keeping the body out of harm's way. This is obvious. But we take the obvious need for physical safety, filter it through our psyches, and then project it onto all our psychological dilemmas.

This truth is utterly simple. The complications arise from all the avenues of escape that have been etched in our minds in various ways. Your way may be similar to someone else's way, but each individual has a particular twist to the tactics of escape.

It is possible to recognize the impulse to escape, and, in the face of that, to stop, to actually turn and meet whatever you have been attempting to escape from. It may be physical, mental, emotional, or political; it may be death or life. It may be your deepest fear, or it may be the deepest bliss. It may mean facing the notion of who you are, and who you are not.

Once the impulse to escape has been recognized, a choice emerges: to say no to the escape and yes to facing the apparent cause of the suffering. The power of choice is the most supreme power of mind, but this choice is of a different order from any other choice ever made. Once the choice to surrender is made, to stop any attempt to escape, then choicelessly, exquisitely, effortlessly, the treasure of your being reveals itself as the truth of who you are. Then you can celebrate the healing of whatever wounds are to be healed, and cry over the wounds that remain. In the midst of both celebration and mourning, you can rest in the truth that is always present.

Yet, until they are investigated, subtle mental arguments have a hold on the choice of surrender: why you cannot stop, or why you should not stop right now, or how you will stop later. Investigation begins once again as you ask yourself what you really want. If what you want is simply to be done with the woundedness, then you will continue to search until you find something that will heal a particular wound, at least temporarily making you feel better. If what you *really* want is the truth of the matter, then you will have all the support necessary to turn and face what you have run from for aeons, what your cellular structure tells you to run from, what all humanity runs from.

There is an immeasurable, unbelievable force that uses every form in your life as a pointer to the support that you need. The support you need is already here! And your role is essential. To be supported, you have to choose to receive the support fully and completely.

I am suggesting that you leap deeply into the core of your being. I know that the experience of the wound can generate the sense that what is in the core of your being is truly horrible. But I have had the great occasion to meet a wide range of people with deep wounds, from psychosis to the usual neuroses that most of us have to deal with. And I have never met anyone who, when they were willing to really tell the truth and face their own suffering, didn't find the beauty and peace of their own essential beingness.

Why not stop and investigate your own impulses toward escape? Not because it is the good thing to do, the holy thing, the right thing, the enlightened thing; it is none of these. It is just simply something you may never have actually experienced. When you do, you find a freshness, an innocence. You will recognize the power and the potential of simply being—not moving toward pleasure, not keeping away pain, not getting another life, and not avoiding the fact of death. In this instant, just be. In the moment of simply being, you find an inner revelation that has the potential to reverberate more and more deeply throughout the mind and body until the mind is no longer preoccupied with justifications for grasping at pleasure or avoiding pain.

There is a treasure that is the truth of your being, and it is saying, "Come in." Perhaps because it has been hidden for so long, you believe that it is dark, ugly, and forbidden, and you have gained much support to not look directly at it. Your whole socialization is about not looking at it. But blessedly, through the power of choice, you can stand outside that socialization and acknowledge a great yearning to know who you are. What a blessed opportunity we all have to support each other in this divine, unimaginable, endless discovery. This possibility is sacred.

I invite you to take a few minutes for direct self-inquiry. To honestly look within and investigate what it is you are running from, what wound you are hoping to heal in order to gain freedom. Let the inquiry reveal the exact mechanisms and strategies of escape. Allow the answers to come forth truthfully, honestly, unedited. Ask yourself this question: *What am I trying to escape?*

You do not need to change or fix whatever is revealed in this questioning. Just recognize the patterns of escape. Experience both the dynamics of the impulse to escape and the possibility of not following that impulse, of bearing the impulse with no story, no strategy, and no preferred outcome. Simply be here, doing nothing. Allow the mind to surrender to the certainty of no escape. Then tell the truth in this moment: Is there still hope of escape, a search for escape, a denial of the inescapability of this moment? If so, just let it all go. Give up every effort to escape, and recognize what truly holds you. Surrender and come to rest in the peace of your being.

# MEETING FEAR  33

At the root of every fixated pattern of suffering is the avoidance of one core emotion: fear. Fear is not the real problem. The problem, and the continuing complication, is all of the mental activity that gets generated in order to avoid really experiencing fear.

Meeting fear is actually simple. It is so simple that there is really no "how to." The skill is in seeing how this meeting is continually avoided. Within this avoidance, all the unconscious, fixated, habitual patterns of suffering are structured.

How is it that you avoid your fear? Do you go numb? Do you deny it? Do you dramatize it? Do you go against it? Do you talk to yourself incessantly? Do you continually fantasize about some future gratification, such as sex, food, money, power, or enlightenment, all as an avoidance of fear?

Right now, you have the capacity to stop avoiding your fear. It is that simple. You can stop telling yourself whatever you are telling yourself, and meet what is here. In meeting any emotion without telling a story about it, you can meet the truth of yourself. More important, you will recognize that this truth has been here all along. Fear passes through it, as do anger, sadness, fixated behavior, despair, emptiness, fullness, ignorance, and enlightenment; they all pass through the truth of yourself. All emotions and mental strategies come and go. *You* are here. You have always been here, unchanging, radiant, pure, and unafraid of any fear that appears.

If all that you desire is to be rid of fear, and you run from it or deny it, fear will haunt you, as anything that you run from will continue to haunt you. In turn, if you chase whatever it is you desire, it will remain just out of reach.

This is also true of the spiritual search. If you want God and you chase God, God will be just out of reach. If you stop and drop every concept of God, you are enfolded in the living presence of God.

The complications that arise in your life reflect either an avoidance of what haunts you or a grasping after what you desire. In an instant of being fully conscious, all complications disappear. Even in the most complicated circumstances, it is possible to be *simply clear.*

Whatever fear may have haunted you all your life, when you stop and you say, "All right, fear, come, I am ready to meet you," you will find that it will start to dart between the corners. If you will send your consciousness after it into every corner, what a discovery you will make!

Once again, you can conduct your own investigation into the anatomy of fear. Where is fear; what does it feel like; what is close to it; what is underneath it? In this moment, if there is no fear present, you can tell yourself some story that will generate fear. Ask yourself directly: *Where is fear?* Maybe you feel it in your heart, maybe in your belly. With your consciousness, drop into the middle of the fear. If a story is still going on in your mind about the fear, let that story go. Let your consciousness fall into the fear that it may have been avoiding for millions of years.

When there is an openness to fear, where can it be found? What a strange creature fear is. It exists only when there is resistance to its existence! When you stop and open to what you have resisted throughout time, you find that fear is not fear. Fear is energy. Fear is space. Fear is the Buddha. It is Christ's heart knocking at your door.

# LETTING GO OF CONTROL 34

S piritual maturity is usually considered a necessity for true awakening, and I am often asked if there is a sign of spiritual maturity. It's true that spiritual maturity is a necessity. This kind of maturity, however, has little to do with how people usually conceive it. It is not related to the number of years you have devoted to spiritual practice, or the number of years you have prayed, or the number of years you have been good. At the most basic level, spiritual maturity has to do with the realization that you are not in control. This is, of course, a shattering realization, because from the age of two, you have believed in the possibility of control, and much of your attention and energy has been funneled into the fight for control.

The desire to be in control, the illusion of being in control, and the hope of being in control are all based on the megalomaniacal belief that you know when and what the outcome should be.

Obviously, you can control many things to a greater or lesser degree, but there is nothing that you can totally control. You can control your bodily functions to a degree, as well as circumstances, thoughts, emotions, position, and survival, but you can never have complete control.

You need no model for letting go. You cannot *do* letting go. Neither is letting go a kind of saintly passivity, not being bothered by anything. The mind is very slippery and can even use the desire to let go as a tactic for control.

Letting go of control is a deeper relaxation, a floating on the ocean. You can become aware of where you are holding on, and you can just let go and allow the ocean to hold you. You can become aware that all your tension and clinging are unnecessary, and then relax and let yourself be supported. In this same way, you can become aware of all the mental and emotional energy that gets exerted in holding on to a particular story, and you can just let it all go. There is a deeper intelligence than the one you use to control, and it is present to be recognized in all lives, at all moments.

Different emotions may arise, including fear, because to let go means you could fall, or you could lose something. Yes! Be willing to lose everything. It is the same as meeting your death. Consciously meeting your death means discovering what cannot be controlled and what is bigger than anyone's power to control; there can be a blessed surrender to that.

If you are searching for a safe, comfortable life, then the freedom I am pointing to is not for you. If you have read this far in the book, then you probably already know that. The invitation to accept the diamond of life is not an invitation to safety and comfort. It is an invitation to live life fully and completely, which is never safe and is often uncomfortable.

Comfort and safety are often searched for because of the belief that they will bring happiness and fulfillment: "If I am just safe enough, then I can relax." But I am talking about recognizing that you can relax right now, even though you aren't completely safe and you never will be. In that understanding is more than safety for the body, mind, or emotions. There is the safety not of any particular form of being, meaning your body or your loved ones' bodies, but of *beingness,* which is eternal.

I would like to make the distinction here between control and support, since much misery is experienced in the belief that one can control, and great joy is experienced in providing support. To support the health of the body, to support the health of the planet, and to support the awakening of all beings is joyous and natural. But to futilely imagine that you can control the health of your body, that you can control the health of the planet or the awakening of all beings, actually creates suffering. This suffering takes attention and energy away from the support you can offer.

In the hope of controlling, your energy and attention are always on some desired outcome, always checking: "Is my body healthy? Are their bodies healthy? Is the planet healthy? Are they waking up? Am I waking up?" Your energy and attention are focused on an end rather than on providing support in this moment. When you shift your attention from control to support, you gain release. You experience fullness as you give up the hope of control, and this fullness can be used to lend support.

The area where you do have some control, and which is too often overlooked, is in the choice of where you put your attention. You can choose to put attention on consciously recognizing what does not need to be controlled and what does not need to be physically well to be truly free, and you can support others in that.

If your attention is on the desire to control, your mind clutches at what you think must happen, should happen, or did happen. That clutching perpetuates suffering. If your desire is to support rather than to control, you will catch fire. The mind will stop its clutching and will begin to open. What follows the natural opening of the mind is the most profound, the most mysterious, the most unspeakable realization.

As you investigate your attempts to control, ask yourself: *What do I try to control?* Be as honest as possible, and then even more honest. Be aware of any defenses to truly seeing, and be willing to drop these defenses. Perhaps you will uncover even more completely what has been hidden behind the closed doors of the mind. Through honest investigation, these doors can open, offering a deep opportunity for surrender.

Open your mind to the possibility that each moment and every circumstance in your life can be a natural investigation into responding without controlling. Do you recognize the difference in responding to what occurs rather than attempting to control? Can you rest in your capacity to respond? Can you rest in your own innate intelligence?

Now you can ask yourself: *What cannot be controlled?* Perhaps through this investigation, you will recognize the enormous energy and mental activity that you have spent unnecessarily in attempting to control what cannot be controlled. Can you open to the possibility of trusting what remains when you let go of any attempt to control?

# GETTING, GIVING, OR SIMPLY BEING

## 35

Another useful question to ask yourself is *What do I want from others?* You can investigate this for yourself and see what is true. I suggest that if what you want from someone else is recognition, love, or respect, you will suffer. On the other hand, if what you want to give to someone else is recognition, love, or respect, you will be happy, in bliss, and free. It is very simple, isn't it? The complication is that you don't truly want to give—first, you want to get.

There are also those who have developed very sophisticated strategies of giving so that they will then get something in return, but they, of course, still suffer.

You can recognize the impulse to get something from others or from life, the hopes that trail that impulse, and how these hopes cement the ongoing experience of yourself as a suffering individual who is not getting enough. If your internal thoughts and fantasies are circling around what you are not getting, you are suffering. All suffering is based on not giving yourself fully to this moment, whether this moment is occurring internally or externally.

In this moment, if you give up the whole pursuit, give up any possibility of getting anything else, ever, then you can discover the bliss of needing nothing, the bliss of simply being. You can discover the underlying bliss of simply being yourself in the face of whatever arises.

When I speak of "being yourself," I am not speaking of being your behavior patterns. I am not speaking of being your thoughts or your emotions. I am speaking of being what cannot be emoted, thought, directed, or defined—the *truth* of yourself.

# THE PRACTICE OF DESIRE

## 36

S omeone once shared with me this very simple yet profound discovery: "If I practice desire, I suffer." What
could be simpler? This essential teaching arose from his
own direct experience.

Certain desires, of course, are totally harmless. If you have the
desire to rest, then rest—the same with eating, speaking, walking,
or reading. But if you have the desire to eat, rest, speak, have sex,
be powerful, or get enlightened, and these desires are neurotic and
cause pain, see that you have the possibility of stopping. You need
the willingness to stop right in the middle of the desire and to burn
in the fire of desire without taking any action to fulfill it.

You may have very sophisticated justifications as to why it is perfectly okay to act on a desire—this time, one more time, for the last
time—and in the middle of these justifications, you can stop. If you

don't give yourself an exit, a kind of crucifixion occurs where an inner resolve arises and says, "Even if it kills me, I am not going to move in this moment." Not moving offers the possibility of discovering the peace of surrender, resurrection, redemption. With that discovery, the bondage of the desire or addictive habit is naturally weakened. It is possible in this moment to totally cut the addiction; at the very least, the link is weakened. Then the next time the impulse arises, you know you have a choice. You know that you are not run by your impulses, no matter how strong they may be.

If you are presently involved in acting out desires—and most people are, to some degree—another way you can approach desire is to consciously watch your involvement with it and then tell the truth. Through conscious awareness, you can watch your mind indulge the addiction, and you can consciously discover your true relationship with it. At least you won't have the usual levels of justification to fall back on.

Allow yourself to fully experience your desire for an object of pleasure. Even though you may know intellectually that it will lead you down the same old path, you may have never fully and consciously acknowledged your attachment to it. There is energy in that infatuation. The pure force of your own desire may subject you to cellular shaking. Be willing to experience the whole of that force and not go numb or dissociate. Experience the burning of being awake and conscious in a bonfire of desire.

Acting out a desire takes some effort. It takes imagining and thinking about what you want or what you have lost. It takes comparing the present moment with some idealized moment of the past or future. It takes attempting to either grasp at something or avoid something. It is a practice. Is it your practice?

What are you spending your lifetime practicing? If you are practicing desire, you are suffering. If you are suffering, see for yourself if you are practicing desire.

# WHAT WILL ENLIGHTENMENT GIVE YOU? 37

Most everyone has experienced how the pursuit of worldly desires often leads to the perpetuation of suffering. From that experience arises the realization that a price is often paid for following those desires. That price is your life energy, focus, and purpose. You can, of course, take pleasure in the attainment of worldly desires, and go through the pain of loss. However, the true deepening of a life doesn't occur until you are willing to see the limitation of worldly desires. Once you see it, you may experience a subtle but deadly transference of worldly desires onto the realm of spiritual desire. The desire for truth, while considered an elevated desire, still leaves you wondering why your suffering continues.

The desire for freedom, love, truth, or God is not a problem. My teacher, Papaji, said that if you desire freedom above all else, then this desire will, in itself, annihilate all other desires; and this is true. This desire swallows all other desires. So the desire for enlightenment is not the problem. The problem is the expectation that enlightenment will give certain results, or look or feel a certain way. From that arise confusion and wondering why, if all one desires is enlightenment, there is still no abiding experience of peace.

I encourage you to really investigate your own mind and see if there is any image of truth, freedom, enlightenment, or God. If there is an image, try this experiment: Let it go. Now see if there is any expectation associated with God, such as, if you are true to God, God will give you perfect health, perfect wealth, eternal happiness, etc. Look into your mind and see if there are expectations that the realization of God or truth will give you some release from life, or some control over life. Now, for the purpose of inquiry, let those expectations go. Surrender them. Give them up. If you are hoping for a particular state of clarity, oceanic bliss, or certainty about your purpose in the world, just let that go so that you are simply *here*. Let everything go. When you have nothing, you have only yourself. And when you truly have only yourself, you are awake to who you truly are.

If you desire to be free, and this desire is not given any form, expectation, or thought, but is just allowed to be, then this true desire reveals the entire known and unknown universe. Every particle is revealed as one, and that one is *you*. The very instant you think your desire for God, freedom, or truth should produce a particular result or look or feel a certain way, you cloud the purity of that true desire.

The challenge in any spiritual seeker's heart, no matter how beautiful and essential the seeking may be, is to stop seeking any *thing* to fulfill that final desire. The challenge is to let your whole life fulfill that desire. You can offer the whole of the rest of your life to that desire without knowing what the result will be, without knowing whether there will be ruination, homelessness, riches, or fame. You can give what you have, which is your life in this moment, to truth, freedom, God.

For another opportunity of self-inquiry, I invite you to ask yourself this question: *What will enlightenment give me?* Depending on how willing you are to tell the truth, the possibilities of this kind of inquiry are limitless. Inquiry has nothing to do with the right answer, but it has everything to do with telling the truth. Take a moment to really consider: What if enlightenment gives you nothing, nothing at all? What if you get not one thing—physical, mental, emotional, or circumstantial? The truth is that enlightenment will not give you one *thing*. Are you willing to bear that truth? If you are, you are free. If you are not, your mind will still be bound to some *thing* you hope will give you freedom.

# ALREADY IMMORTAL  38

Whether consciously or unconsciously, most humans actively endeavor to keep whatever it is they like—their youth, health, pleasures, understanding, power, lovers, bliss, and so on. Of course, along with attempting to keep what they like, they attempt to keep away what they do not like—aging, illness, confusion, helplessness, loneliness, misery, and so on. The mental effort to keep what is subject to loss, what will be lost, is the basis for most suffering. Ultimately comes the attempt to keep death away.

To discover real freedom, it can be very useful to investigate what you are trying to keep or what you are afraid to lose. Self-investigation is the act of finally meeting any force that drives your thoughts and strategies of mind. That force always comes down to the fear of loss.

With some degree of spiritual ripening, you can easily recognize the futility of trying to keep what you will surely lose. It is not difficult to remember that you have had moments of health, pleasure, understanding, power, romantic love, and maybe even ecstasy—and yet those moments have been lost. When desired events or things are lost, usually the search reincarnates with the hope of getting something even greater, something that cannot be lost this time.

By the time I met my teacher, I had finally recognized that all my accomplishments and all my powers were still subject to loss, and the attempt to keep them was the basis of my suffering. I saw that I needed a constant level of effort to maintain what I thought I had, to strive to get whatever I hoped I might still get, and to keep at bay whatever might take away what I thought I had. This effort takes a surprising amount of attention. Much of the mental maintenance of the supposed status quo goes on subconsciously—monitoring, evaluating, ranking, comparing, and judging, over and over, day and night. The tragedy in all of this effort is in overlooking what is already eternal, immortal, and can never be lost.

You may have heard certain spiritual statements such as "Silence is always here," "Awareness is always here," or "Awareness is who you are." You may have experienced at least a glimpse of these truths. But a glimpse of truth will also be lost because it is still an experience. All experience appears, exists for some time, and then disappears. Usually the mind then scrambles to get that experience back, or to attain another, better, bigger experience.

Once this mental cycle goes around many hundreds or even thousands of times, a certain disillusionment can set in. This disillusionment is necessary, because it generates the field required for the maturation of the mind. A mature mind has the willingness and fortitude to tell the truth. And the truth is ruthless and relentless. The truth is that you *will* lose your youth, you *will* lose your health, you *will* lose your pleasure, your understanding, your lovers, your mate, your children, and finally your senses and your body. You will lose everything. Although deep inside you know that this is true, there is usually a subconscious, desperate grasping at the hope, "Maybe not me. Maybe not!"

Eventually, all will be lost. At some point, unknown in time, your life will come to an end, and with it all your relationships and experiences, all your defeats, victories, accumulations, and attainments. *Everything* will be gone. This is true for everyone.

In the past, it was a great rarity when someone stepped forth to speak of what is eternal, of what cannot be lost, of what is already the truth of who we are. In general, the great, rare beings who speak of this have been misunderstood. The way that most people heard them was based on the hope, "If I get what this great being is saying, then I will have what this great being has, and it can never be taken away from me." Then all energy was directed toward trying to get something or trying to figure something out. I invite you to do neither. I invite you to simply investigate directly within yourself to see what is true.

If, for one moment, you will allow yourself the experience of losing everything, *really* losing everything, you can tell the radical truth of what is always present. You can understand *directly*, for yourself, what those great beings were pointing to. You can understand the scriptures and the sutras as the overflowing of your own experience, not as something to work toward, but as a song of what is eternally present.

Eternal life is present for you now. You have the capacity to realize this because *you* are what realizes *itself*. What was rare in the past need not be rare now. It is a horribly limited superstition to believe that since self-realization has been rare, it must continue to be rare. This is a thought-form that keeps your mind encased in denial and hope, encased in the continual overlooking of what is already immortal and present in this moment, now and always. This immortality is what your body, personality, and character traits appear and disappear in, while it remains eternally present as the core of your being. The truth of who you are is both one and all. All form appears in you. All emotions appear in you. All phenomena appear and disappear in you.

The attention, energy, and time that have been spent trying to "get" something can be released, set free. This freed energy can be used for deeper self-exploration. Your mind can be used for a deeper exploration of what is already immortal, already presently here, already the truth of who you are—eternal life.

# THE HEART OF
## SELF-BETRAYAL 39

P eople have spoken to me about the grief of experiencing a moment of purely knowing the truth of their being, then having the mind turn away from it. Most people want to get rid of that grief because it feels painful. If you honestly look in your life, I believe you will see that at the root of most of the mind's activities is the attempt to rid oneself of this ancient grief.

We have all experienced the grief of losing something, a beloved one, or a precious object. But even deeper than that grief is the grief of recognizing the betrayal of the truth of ourselves. Rather than actually experiencing this self-betrayal, we usually get very busy fabricating proof that we are not betraying ourselves. We busily gather power, pleasure, or knowledge to prove that we are not really betraying ourselves, that we really are okay. But this grief, this divine sadness, is very important. It is a great, painful gift from the emotional body, and we deal with it in at least a couple of ways.

One approach to the grief of self-betrayal is to dramatize it, to make it into a dance, a song, or a play, glorifying the sadness and the pain. Another common way is to deny the grief, to push it down out of sight, to numb or deaden ourselves. It doesn't matter which we choose, because the grief remains. The loss of being true to ourselves is still present.

We spend much time and energy accumulating powers, objects, and knowledge in order to avoid experiencing this core grief. Perhaps this avoidance is really the genesis of human suffering.

All of us have the potential to actually meet the extreme pain of turning from the truth of ourselves, to actually accept this gift. I assume that if you are reading this book, you have had some instant of pure and perfect alignment with the truth of who you are and a resulting moment of absolute bliss. Whether that moment happened before any conscious spiritual search or through years of arduous spiritual practice, it was a moment of supreme surprise.

That perfect moment was extremely pleasurable, and you have wanted to hold that pleasure. You want to learn what to do to keep it safe. After attempting that for some time, you realize that you have lost it once again.

The pain of recognizing that we have turned away from the truth of ourselves leads to a great cry, a wail, a tearing of the heart. We very busily find ways to distract ourselves from our own sense of loss. In the Western world, in particular, we scurry and frantically search for something to take away the echo of the loss. But nothing does. Then through the promise of the spiritual path, and perhaps through grace, we again discover the surprise of our own innocent heart, open and in alignment with the truth of our being. And once again, the desire usually arises at that very moment not to lose it, not to throw it away again. This is yet another temptation of the mind. What follows this temptation is a simulation of what has been gained, a blissful attitude or a happy face, which may be preferable to other attitudes. But it is still a lie, still a betrayal.

It is possible to lay bare your soul's deep grief without dramatizing it or denying it, to recognize that this longing is an echo of what originates purely and absolutely in the core of your being.

I am not talking about emotionalism. Emotionalism is generally an avoidance of this deepest of emotions. It is a way of dancing around grief rather than truly meeting it. I am not saying to tell yourself some sob story. That, too, is a way of avoidance. I am also not asking you to slap a happy face on top of the ache. This ache has a divine purpose. If you will meet it, this divine ache will return your attention to this present moment where perfect alignment with the truth of who you are can always be found.

It is very important to acknowledge the sense of loss, suffering, and deep grief in that experience. Then it is important to see how this sense of loss gets covered by activities, distractions, addictions, or objects in an attempt to fill the emptiness. All these activities are really to avoid what is perceived as the final loss: death, which we fear will forever separate us from what we have glimpsed to be eternally alive.

Everything that is born will die. This is a stark and ruthless truth. It is also a divine truth and a doorway to what is eternal. The activities of the mind serve to escape that truth, to keep death away. This is a natural aspect of mind, designed to protect the body from death. It is natural to all life forms, and it is not a problem unless the instinct goes unmet. Unmet, it has the power to keep all deep experience of the unknown unmet. It has the power to prevent true intimacy with yourself and life itself. It has the power to keep your life's experience only on the surface, while terror of the depths keeps the mind dancing in avoidance.

This dance is one of suffering, misery, and frantic absurdity. If you are at least somewhat exhausted from it, it is a good sign. In your willingness to keep dancing, to keep going and going, you lose the ability to stop and rest. To stop and rest means to turn and face what has been avoided by the dancing: the grief of turning away from the awakened innocent heart of your own being.

# CONSCIOUS INNOCENCE 40

I have often heard from people that after a powerful opening glimpse of the unimaginable truth of their being, the demons of the past seem to arise more strongly than ever. Rather than the openness and innocence of "What is this now?" the response is often something like "Why is this bothering me again? Why don't these things just disappear? What is wrong with *me* that I don't experience permanent liberation?" On one hand, there is misery and suffering, and on the other hand, innocence and openness. These "hands" are the polarities of the mind. True innocence is the innate capacity of the heart to openly meet whatever is appearing when it appears, and to see it truthfully for what it is. I guarantee that most everything is not what it appears to be on the surface, but in order to discover a deeper truth, what appears must be met fully in innocence. Not the learned innocence of "but I'm innocent," but the natural openness of innocently not knowing.

True innocence is the capacity to directly experience what is here right now, without any demands that it look, act, or feel differently.

Innocence is openness, the willingness to see and to trust, even if what appears seems absolutely untrustworthy. True innocence is not naiveté, nor is it delusion. However, it involves vulnerability. The willingness to be innocent is the willingness to be hurt. This willingness to be vulnerable is what the term "spiritual warrior" really means. Vulnerability takes more courage than being cynical, strong, or powerful. It takes courage to be open, innocent, and willing to be hurt.

Because of the nature of extremely close relationships, especially between parents, children, lovers, and partners, hurt is often experienced. So what? Hurt may feel like the end of the world, but it's not. Hurt hurts. The degree to which you are willing to be hurt, not *wanting* to be hurt but *willing* to be hurt, is the degree to which you are willing to love, be loved, and be taught by love. Love can be your teacher, though it never teaches withdrawal from experiencing hurt. Other people are not the source of your hurt; the source of hurt is the *fact* that you love. Trust the love. If love is to hurt you, then let it hurt you fully. Let it annihilate you. Let your heart break open so that an even deeper love can be revealed.

Most everything we do is to avoid vulnerability. We dress up in grown-up clothes, and play at doing grown-up work, in an attempt to escape the defenseless innocence associated with childhood. But innocence is not limited to children. It is possible for you as an adult to be consciously vulnerable and innocent. You can *consciously* hurt. You can *consciously* suffer. When you suffer consciously, suffering is revealed not to be what you thought. In conscious suffering, you are no longer fighting the suffering. You are consciously present in it. Then suffering itself reveals the Buddha, Christ's heart, God revealing Itself to you on the mountain. If suffering is met as it appears, then suffering is discovered not to be suffering. But the intention is not to meet suffering to get rid of it. The innocent intention is to meet suffering as it is, even if it means feeling hurt.

Most people are more afraid of having their feelings hurt than they are of having their bodies hurt. But the willingness to be hurt is crucial. Without the willingness to be hurt, there is no willingness to love, no willingness to die, no willingness to live, no willingness to *be*.

It is easy to see from your own life experience that no matter how much you try to run away from hurt, you still experience it. To stop the running, to turn and experience what is chasing you, open and unprotected, you have to be willing to be free. Are you willing to be free?

You can examine your life and see for yourself what you are running from, what you are trying to escape. It may be very subtle. But just in the seeing of it, there is the possibility of a deeper opening.

Everywhere I've spoken with people, I have heard this statement: "I want truth, God, and realization more than anything else—

why don't I have it?" When you honestly want truth, God, and realization more than anything else, you realize it is already here. People don't realize it is already here only because they still want it on their terms.

Look into your life and see what stands in the way of fully and permanently realizing the truth of your being. See if perhaps you find the mindset of having it your way, on your terms, not wanting to feel this, or to see that, or to know the deeper truth. Then see if it is actually possible to feel it, to see it, to know it.

As a gateway to the experience of conscious suffering, and as a means of opening to vulnerability and true innocence, you can ask yourself this question: *What hurt am I unwilling to experience?* Do not look for the "right" spiritual answer, or lie to yourself, but simply open to what this kind of inquiry can reveal. The intention is not to fix or change the hurt, but just to see what is true.

Can you sense the energy it takes to avoid feelings of hurt? Review the ways you try to avoid hurt, what habits of mind you use to avoid it. Be willing to see the repeating patterns and to experience the price you pay for the avoidance, all of the time and energy that you invest in avoidance. Just in this moment, what if you simply open to it all, avoiding nothing, welcoming all?

Are you willing to trust love rather than your mind's protection from hurt? If you are willing, then you will taste the possibility of

THE DIAMOND IN YOUR POCKET

living a life of love and conscious innocence. This is possible for everyone. Love is the teacher. If you are willing to surrender to love rather than trying to control it, love teaches you who you are.

# SURRENDERING TO LOVE 41

Many people have trouble with the word *love*. Love, as most of us have known it, can be sentimental, potentially messy, and most definitely out of control. And yet, love is what we crave. There is often a love/hate relationship with the idea of love, most likely stemming from our experiences as children when we loved helplessly. We projected love out onto our loved ones—our mothers, fathers, brothers, or sisters—and at some point, found our loved ones to be unreliable. We confused their actions with love and concluded that love was not trustworthy.

People are definitely not trustworthy, because, in general, they are very busy protecting their story of who they think they are. Since they are mostly involved in their story, they can only give a certain amount of love before they start wondering, "Well, when do I get mine?" And since love has been identified as being connected with another person, this sets up a whole continuation of distrust around love. But love is not a person. Love is the individual, collective, and universal soul. Love is God. Love is truth. Love is beauty. Love is peace. Love is self. To *know* yourself, to surrender to the truth of yourself, is to surrender to love.

Many people are aware of their resistance, and they want to surrender, but they don't know *how*. The only actual barrier to surrender is in not seeing the underlying story you are telling yourself about the danger of surrendering everything to love. And the degree to which you hold back surrendering everything to love is the degree to which you suffer. The degree to which you try to maintain the story about who you think you are is the degree to which you feel isolated from love. Until you realize, "I want truth, which is love, more than anything," you will experience yourself as separate from love. Love is the constant. Love is not an aspect of truth. Truth, God, and self are aspects of love.

What is the worst that could happen if you surrender to love? What we seem to fear the most is the broken heart. Yet the very unwillingness for the heart to be broken *is* the broken heart. The tragedy and the irony is that in order to avoid a broken heart, people live in a state of broken-heartedness. In the willingness to have the heart be broken a million, trillion, zillion times, true love is revealed.

Let the whole world break your heart every instant of the remainder of your life. Then this life can be lived in service to love. It does not mean you stay in abusive relationships. It means only to stay true to that which is always true to you, and that is love. Anything else is a story. If the story is never investigated, your whole life is lived on the assumption that the story is real, and that your heart, your soul, and your love need to be protected. But that assumption is actually a denial of your heart, your soul, your love. It is a denial of self-love.

The great good news is that love is free and it has not gone anywhere. In all these aeons that you have been hiding from love, love is still here, it is still open, it is still waiting for your commitment, still waiting for you to say, "Yes, I give my life to the truth of love. I vow to let love live this life as it will, for better or worse, for richer or poorer."

Through honest self-investigation, it is possible to see why you may not be surrendering to love, and to see that you actually have the choice to surrender. It is a way to let the unconscious storylines become conscious, the unknown become known. Ask yourself this question: *Why is it dangerous to surrender to love?* Not why is it *right* to surrender to love, or why is it *good* to surrender to love, but why is it *dangerous* to surrender to love?

Let your individual consciousness drop down into the source of consciousness, into the space where all the reasons and justifications for resisting surrender are seen simply as stories, as something made up that you can very easily let go. Allow all the stories, all the defenses, to be seen for what they are. Are any of these stories worth keeping? What is the cost to your life?

The love that you search for everywhere is already present within you. It may be evoked by any number of people or events. A mountain can evoke this love. A sunset can evoke this love. But finally, you must realize you *are* this love. The source of all love is within you.

# PART FOUR

---

## CHOOSING

## PEACE

# TAKING RESPONSIBILITY 42

When you are called home, when you are somehow struck by the absolutely mysterious and irrevocable desire to know the truth of who you are, then you must be willing to put aside every story of separation. Every story of separation is a story of war.

Human beings have been making war in every culture for a very long time. Culture is a reflection of the individual mind, and the individual mind is a reflection of the cultural mind. Since you are reading this, I assume you are interested in peace in your own mind. You are not waiting for *them* to make peace. This is good news, because war is fought to get *others* to do it *our* way so that *we* can live in peace. When you stop waiting for *them,* and instead shift your attention to your own mind, then you can recognize the tendency toward war in your own mind, the tendencies of totalitarianism, hate, revenge, and holding on. And you can recognize the suffering that those tendencies continue to deliver.

Somehow, in the face of it all, you find you want peace. You are sick and tired of the war within your own mind. You may even express it in a conscious prayer, a plea for help, for understanding, for deliverance, for grace.

Grace is here now. It is knocking at your door. You have a chance to be at peace in this moment. You only need to accept the invitation of your own heart, right now, regardless of outer or inner circumstances, and let yourself sink into the peace of your innermost being.

Unless all of us take the responsibility for our own inner peace, the wars will continue. We cannot wait any longer for someone else to change. We cannot wait for someone else to forgive us so that we can then forgive them. We cannot wait for someone else to say they are sorry. Peace cannot be postponed.

Recognize that to whatever degree the war is going on in your own mind, it is based on one thing: the firm belief that you are a separate entity, separate from your parents, your children, your lover, or your enemy.

All wars are based upon the ignorance of our true nature and the illusion of separation. When you firmly believe that you are separate from the totality, separate from peace, separate from love, you protect yourself. That protection takes many forms involving personal and territorial identification. The horror is that if what you are protecting is the thought of who you are, it does not, in reality, even exist. It is only a thought, and whenever a thought is honestly investigated, it is found to have no inherent reality. Yet this thought of who you are has immeasurable power, because it becomes the filter of all experiences of reality.

When you look through tinted glass, reality takes on that tint. It isn't that reality is tinted. The tinted glass mediates and distorts reality. People fight for the distortion that this "I," as an individual or as a group, is separate from all other beings. And yet that "I" is actually nothing! It is a made-up story. Yet, in the belief that the story is reality, there is colossal tragedy and suffering. When this "I" that is assumed to be real and separate is examined by consciousness, it is discovered to be none other than consciousness itself.

As a conscious human being, you have the opportunity to discover that never, not even for an instant, is it possible to be separate from consciousness, from the source of everything, from God. Once you discover this directly, you then broadcast it with every breath you take. Whether you speak of this discovery or you never speak again, you will broadcast it through the natural radiance of your being. In your willingness to take that chance, to accept that invitation, you will naturally share that peace everywhere.

At this point in time, in this theatre of consciousness, you have the opportunity to discover what is deeper than "human" being, what is before human being. That "being-ness" is actually the source of human being. It is the source of plant being, animal being, sentient being, and insentient being. That beingness is alive with intelligence, with presence, and it wants to know itself in you so that it can know itself everywhere.

# CHOOSING PEACE
## OVER PROBLEMS

43

I n the interest of peace, perhaps it is time to take an honest look at what you consider to be "problems" in your life. In order to even reflect on a problem, you will see that first you have to go into memories of the past to generate a story of the supposed problem. This is a moment of choice, and this choice is present in every moment of your life.

Generally, we choose to remember the past to recreate our problems. If we choose not to regenerate them, what does that mean about their importance? How can we know we have learned the lesson? We have an investment in the problem's importance, so we go back to the past to conjure it up again. This is called "rebirth." This is the choice to be reborn with the same problems, stories, and miseries, day by day. Once we are aware of that choice, we have the possibility of recognizing exactly what is required to keep any problem alive. It is necessary to invest time, effort, and energy on what "was" to keep feeding the importance of the problem.

We search for answers to alleviate our problems and to end our suffering, but the search follows the rebirth, a rebirth that we have actually chosen. The choice we often make is to be reborn as the sufferer, rather than simply be here as nobody, as nothing.

The willingness to be nothing, to defend against nothing, can lead to exceedingly intense feeling. A great fear can arise: "I could really disappear here, and then the whole of my life will be of no actual importance." But you have to understand that this is going to happen anyway. You really *will* disappear at some point, and even though you may make great contributions in your life, finally, they too will disappear.

So the question becomes: Are you willing, at least for this moment, to not be reborn? If you are, then you can recognize what *is* unborn, what remains alive without story, without suffering, without problem. Recognize what remains alive, and let its spaciousness, its peace, be revealed as your own heart. You can recognize it as yourself, having nothing to do with birth or death. If you are willing to be true to that recognition, then rebirth is not a problem, because then your story, your "problems," are consciously recognized as appearing in the vast intelligence of who you truly are. Then you know yourself as essentially free of any past. The past can be welcomed, can be learned from, and can be appreciated in its full spectrum of beauty and horror.

# VICTIM NO LONGER  44

No matter what the world is reflecting, whether circumstances are beautiful or terrifying, if your internal story is one of victimhood, you will suffer. It is very simple. If you are quite certain that you aren't telling yourself a story of victimization, and yet you continue to suffer, then I suggest you are lying to yourself. You are telling yourself some thread of an ancient story of how you have been wronged. Whether it is a story of how God, or your parents, or circumstances have wronged you, or how you have wronged yourself, it is all a story of you being the victim. Even the most violent aggressors, when the superficial layer of aggression is cracked, have a story of having been wronged. Striking out in anger or revenge always involves a story of victimization.

Seeing how this victim story plays out in your own life is an important step toward realizing true freedom. When you really see it, you see that it has to be recreated each time it plays. It may surface in your mind through momentum, but to play it through takes energy, attention, belief, emotion, and some kind of masochistic pleasure in the pain. Yes, it's shocking! To see this operating within your own mind can be quite disturbing.

The willingness to realize the truth of yourself, the willingness to be free, is the willingness to no longer be a victim—regardless of pain, circumstances, or the actions of others. To stop being a victim doesn't mean to trivialize the horror in your life, to deny it, gloss over it, or repress it. It means that you can fully meet whatever appears. You don't have to hide, run, justify, wail, curse, or moan. You can just meet life as it is.

Are you willing to let your stories of victimization go? Are you willing to let all those horrible aggressors go unpunished? At a certain point, you have to be willing to just call it off. Yes, there has been horrible suffering, and you have been on both ends of it. You have perpetuated it, and you have experienced it directed at you. Are you willing to end it? You are free to suffer, and you are free to stop suffering. No one can end it but you. That is where your freedom is.

Conscious freedom is the freedom to meet suffering consciously, and then consciously choose to let it go. The bondage is in being unaware of the choice. You can choose to be free, or you can choose to suffer. It is up to you.

# THE POWER OF
## FORGIVENESS 45

Everyone has experienced the sweet release of forgiveness, as well as the hard coldness of not forgiving. You know the difference, and you know the investment in the story that keeps a lack of forgiveness in place. You also know the relief when you actually forgive and let go of the burden.

Our parents were not perfect. They consciously or unconsciously did things that were harmful to us, as our grandparents did things that were harmful to our parents. Our lovers, our children, our governments, and our competing tribes have harmed us. Now is the time to forgive.

Horrible things are continually being done all over the planet, in our own individual minds and in the collective mind. To forgive these horrors does not necessarily mean to forget. You can forgive and let go without forgetting. A huge learning and humbling occurs when you are willing to see the story of humanity in all its horrors. Yet you can also recognize how much effort is needed to hang on to the story. You can see that all the effort and attention put into hanging on are actually a meditation on not forgiving. The stories continue to replay, with an obsession over what should have been done or what might be done again. Continuing to replay the story saps your energy. It is exhausting.

I honor the need to remember and to witness the horror that has been done and is still being done. But usually we bring to that memory more hatred, suffering, and misery, which ensures even more hatred, suffering, and misery.

After the war in Yugoslavia in 1999, I saw a news clip of a home video filmed by a man who said he was making the video so that his children could see what had been done to them, and so that they would never forget or forgive. The horrors occurring at that time were themselves in retaliation for what one group of people had previously done to the other.

The futility and the waste of this kind of tribal warfare is going on within our own minds as well: "I'm not going to let go of what *they* did to *me,* because it was *wrong.*"

Yes, wrongs have been done and are still being done. There is no need to forget or deny the wrongs that have been done both to you and by you, but you can let go of suffering over them. "Forgive them, for they know not what they do" is the truth. Any war that is going on because of what happened yesterday is the result of ignorance, of holding on to some idea of revenge.

It is very tempting to hold on to these kinds of views because there is some pleasure in it, and that pleasure must be recognized. It is the pleasure of egoic righteousness.

When you are unwilling to forgive, and you are holding on to a story of your suffering and who did it to you, you are cursing them, whether consciously or unconsciously. You must be willing to stop the karma with yourself, be willing to say, "No, this time it goes no further than me." This is the willingness to be at peace. The willingness to forgive is a natural outgrowth of the willingness to be free, and gives you the clarity to recognize the temptation to hold on.

I once called my mother on Mother's Day. My mother was a sarcastic and mean alcoholic. Alcohol was poisoning her, shifting her whole personality. I had had some space from her for years, and I decided one year that I would call her on Mother's Day and simply lie to her and tell her what a great mother she was. She was old and sick, and she didn't have many years left, so why not? I called her and told her what a great mother she had been to me, and as the words came out of my mouth, they were true. I didn't mean she had treated me well, because she hadn't. I didn't mean her intentions were great; sometimes they were, and sometimes they weren't.

But as I told her that she had been a good mother, my life experience was finally augmented by my relationship with this very difficult woman. My difficulty with my mother finally contributed to the richness of my life. In that sense, she was indeed a good mother.

What a relief there was in telling her this. Concurrently, my ability to forgive myself for having hated her for so many years arose. It was such a simple act. I had no idea I would see such ramifications of healing.

Finally, to be able to forgive this whole experience of humanity, with all its functions, drives, aggressions, and desires, is to recognize what is untouched by any of that, what remains pure, innocent, and free even in the grossest of stories.

In our desire to hold on to revenge, we actually keep ourselves from the experience of freedom. As with everything else, in our desire to hold on to one thing, we keep something else away. In the desire to give something, we actually receive.

You can inquire directly within: *What am I not willing to forgive?* As you do this, you find another opportunity to bring to consciousness what is not consciously seen, what might still be holding your mind in bondage. No effort is needed here, only the willingness to be completely honest.

Once you have honestly seen what you are not willing to forgive, you might also find it helpful to ask yourself: *What am I willing to forgive?*

Recognize forgiveness and savor it for a moment. It is important not to *force* anything, just to welcome all into the heart of consciousness. Can you forgive? Can you accept forgiveness?

# NO END TO OPENING 46

O ne of the dangers I have seen of the so-called "spiritual life" is the ego's attempt to use spiritual life to escape heartbreak, difficulty, and continued patterns of hatred, revenge, and war—to escape the idea of a hell. The desire for transcendence becomes bigger than the willingness to let the heart open to it *all*, the totality of human beauty as well as the totality of human catastrophe. When you are willing to fully experience the hopelessness and the horror of being human, the eternal potential for living life in truth is freed.

The readiness to be free means being ready to see that there is no escape from any aspect of life, and to stop fantasizing about any future escape. Fantasies of escape can take myriad forms, including an infantile image of heaven or enlightenment. The willingness to be free is the willingness to actually be right here in the midst of it all. The greater the willingness, the greater the capacity for being even more fully present; the realization finally comes that there is no need for escape. Whatever appears here can be borne here, regardless of what the mind imagines it can or cannot bear. The madness that is feared in the prospect of meeting whatever is here is actually fostered by continually trying to escape. In meeting whatever is here, fully and completely, is the potential for the unspeakable, indefinable, unteachable revelation of truth.

Most people spend most of their lives involved in personal suffering—"What happened to me, what may happen to me, what should be happening to me, what should not be happening to me." Obviously, a much larger story of suffering is occurring in the world today. It calls for us to resolve our personal stories and turn our attention to the world story. If you have been at all ready to face the horrors of the personal story, then it is possible for you now to face the world story. And that, too, is just a beginning.

Certainly, the patterns of war are familiar, whether from this century or any other, this culture or any other. There may be pain freshly experienced in the current horrors happening all over the world, and a desire may arise to want to know what to do. I invite you to meet these horrors, freshly, innocently, surrendering everything to that same force that calls you home.

Of course, you can remain faithful to conditioned existence, where you have learned to *know* exactly what should be, or you can find agreement and support for intellectual understanding, which might even give you an experience of peace. Perhaps with intellectual understanding, you won't be bothered by messy tears and emotions.

The more you stop struggling to get out, the more pain you will experience, but also the more joy you will experience. This is the paradox that the mind cannot resolve, although there are many strategies to resolve it. We have all learned great powers of mind. These powers include techniques of denial and indulgence, all revolving around the central technique of lying. But the power of the mind is only needed for protection and attack. If you are willing to bear it all, you have no need of anything but surrender, telling the truth, and being yourself.

The invitation to stop is a radical invitation. It is the invitation to stop *only* in this moment. It is not the invitation to stop for the rest of your life, to never leave your house, to never tell a story, or to never think again. It is the invitation to stop everything and, just for this moment, *be.*

One of Papaji's most profound teachings is to "wait and see." To "wait" is active and open, and the seeing *is* the waiting. It is to see the impulses of the mind, to see the ancient programming embedded in the cellular structure to *know* what to do, what action to take. Just wait and see. Rest nakedly in not knowing. True lasting discovery is not something you have heard or read about. It is your own direct experience.

Until now, we have opted for trusting our minds, language, images, and ideas, rather than trusting the spaciousness from which all arises. What an opportunity is available now to trust the unknown spaciousness of the heart. What a time.

Yes, there is beauty in these times. Opening and awakening are happening all over the world. All of the horror, grief, outrage, and anguish are not separate from that awakening. The more we accept opening to whatever is appearing, the greater are the challenges. The more we see, the more our heart breaks. In our surrender to the heart broken open, all the way, there is freedom. In our attempts to not feel the pain of the heart breaking, in our attempts to finally *know* what should be, there is bondage.

# DROPPING THE LAYERS
## OF INSULATION

47

A s a culture, we in the West have spent a lot of energy attempting to insulate ourselves from the horror and the suffering in the world. And, in fact, many of us have been protected from what other people on the planet have to deal with daily: the immediacy of suffering and death, the immediacy of change, of one government falling to another government, of repression and the accompanying lack of physical freedoms. But in one unexpected instant on September 11, 2001, the insulation of the United States, with its affluence and its protection, its illusory cocoon of safety and separation, was penetrated by the reality of the world's politics.

Most people spend their lives trying to create security for themselves, setting up insurance plans and retirement plans, and living in certain locations and communities. This obsession with security is all based on the lie that we can control the events of life. Certain events, like the terrorist attacks of September 11, obviously penetrate that lie. It must be seen that no matter how much we try to be secure—even to the degree of selling our souls, of living false, loveless lives for security—in any unexpected instant, everything can disappear. If we can face the inherent danger of life, if we can face death, then we can live freely. Freely does not mean stupidly. Perhaps you will still initiate insurance and retirement plans, but you will not be bound by the false hope that any plan can ever truly protect your body, your family, or your nation.

The rawness of our time can seem unbearable. We have been trained to cover it over and to push it aside so that we can get on with our business, get on with our shopping, get on with the pretense that nothing is ever going to happen to harm us. Concurrently, there is a deep quickening to know the truth of peace, to be true to that truth, and to have one's life serve that.

As horrible as the calamities happening all over the planet are, they can serve to penetrate our day-to-day trance, revealing a portal into experiencing right now, in this moment, what is really here. If fear is present, then there is the opportunity to experience that fear fully, and to discover what is deeper than the fear. Whatever is here—despair, anger, frustration, or hopelessness—the opportunity is to not cover it with our usual day-to-day conditioning of denial or sublimation, but to face it, to meet it, to directly experience it.

The truth is, whatever insulation we have constructed against the world is actually the insulation around our own hearts. That insulation is built on the lack of recognition that the peace in our hearts is actually inclusive of horror. We don't normally recognize this, because we haven't been taught that we can stop for a moment and discover the peace at the core of our own being. We most definitely have been taught how to armor and to insulate.

My invitation to you is to drop all insulation, and to fully experience the heartbreak and the suffering, whether it is your own individual suffering or the suffering going on all over the planet. I encourage you to experience this suffering fully, without doing anything to get away from it, to fix it, or to change it. Simply experience it, just for a moment.

Possibly you feel called in some way to help end world suffering. There is nothing wrong with trying to end world suffering, but any action to try to *get* peace or *make* peace is ultimately futile. History demonstrates this futility. You cannot get what is already here, but you can recognize the peace that is already present within you and be in solidarity with that peace, regardless of whatever action is taken. You may be a political activist, an ecological activist, or a peace activist, but that activism is very different if it results in *having* peace rather than trying to *get* peace. When action arises out of peace, its spontaneity and rapport with the world allow the heart to be broken again and again, without any need to insulate it from the breaking. With each breaking can come an even deeper recognition of what remains unbreakable, and this is the source of compassion and the source of all lasting help in the world.

Certainly, people have different affinities. Some people are not interested in action of any kind, while others are interested in action of all kinds. Regardless of your affinity, I am pointing to that which is the source of it all, and that source is here right now. It is not something that you will get somewhere else or sometime in the future.

It is possible to trust that right action can come from the unknown stillness of your being. You have learned not to trust this stillness, because you are afraid that you will just lie on the couch all day. And you might just do that. Your body is probably exhausted anyway.

Whatever emotions come up in the enormity of space, let them come up. You don't have to push them away. You can meet them in the spaciousness. Consciousness can meet emotion. You do not need to fight the emotions that may arise, or deny the spaciousness. There is a force that is bigger than any emotion, any individual mind, any governmental mind, any "us" and "them" mentality, and that force is trustworthy.

I don't know if we, as a human species, will be extinct in the next few hundred years, or even if the planet itself will be extinct. But I do know that we can spend whatever time we have left in the deepest inquiry into the truth of who we are, and we can trust that inquiry to lead to appropriate action or non-action. In that openness of inquiry, we can trust also that we will make mistakes, and that we have both the capacity to recognize mistakes and the courage to make amends. We don't have to know what the plan is, but we do have to be true to peace, to take responsibility for choosing to overlook what is already at peace. We have learned how to armor, to lie, and to protect ourselves. Yet deeper, closer than any strategy we have learned, the peace remains. It is here right now.

It is possible to dismantle the insulation and untie the knot, to bust through the lie so that true peace can be recognized and the love that is the essential self of all beings is recognizable in all. It is astonishingly simple. Just in this moment, be still. In this stillness, discover for yourself if there is a bottom to the stillness. Then the horrors of the world no longer need to be defended against. The stillness of being can meet them all. Then the love that is a further dimension of this stillness can be extended to both the victims and the victimizers of violence.

What will happen in your life if you accept the invitation to stillness cannot be known. What can be known is you will have a larger capacity to truly meet whatever appears. The freedom of this revelation is extraordinary, yet it is also very ordinary. When you meet world suffering, *any* suffering, *all the way through,* it reveals the true, natural, spacious compassion of your own heart.

# THE TREASURE
## WITHIN DESPAIR 48

If you feel a deep outrage at the suffering you see around you, investigate the root of your outrage. Go all the way into it with your consciousness, without expressing it or acting it out, denying or repressing it. You may experience another emotion under the outrage. Relatively speaking, outrage is superficial. Under the outrage is often a profound despair at the endless cruelty, seemingly everywhere you look.

I invite you to let your heart break deeper than it has ever been broken so that it can see even more of what is going on. If you get to this point of despair, right now, as you read this, allow your consciousness to fall into the core of this despair. Despair is the one emotion that is most avoided. To meet despair means to let go of any story about despair. Simply meet it in innocence so that you can discover what is at the core.

Then you can discover that your despair holds a treasure from the depths of yourself.

Most people would prefer to get rid of their despair so that they only experience bliss. But this is a form of fascism—spiritual fascism—which wants only bliss. Bliss feels good and makes you happy, while despair feels bad, and you want it out of your sight. This tendency gives rise to the totalitarian point of view, whether material or spiritual.

Are you willing to invite despair, which you have hated, which you have sent away, into your heart? Are you willing to see that hating despair and sending it away don't get rid of it? Are you willing to say, "Okay, despair, come in, let me meet you as you are"? You don't have to. You can hang on to your despair or outrage forever, and you can even pass them on to others. When you do, you feel in alignment with the outrage. You can actually feel pleasure being aligned with outrage, and this alignment is even appropriate at certain moments. But can you also be in alignment with what you discover at the core of despair? That core is the truth of your being. If you are in alignment with that, you are in alignment with all. Nothing is excluded.

There is so much unexperienced grief in the closed heart, but the heart broken open sets grief free. When you meet your own pain, grief, or despair all the way, you discover that each holds the gem of truth.

Confusion arises because certain spiritual teachings say that detachment from the world is necessary for enlightenment. The concept of detachment can be confused with release from pain, a way of numbing so that you don't have to experience the pains of life. If you are not willing to fully experience the pains of love, the pains of the heart breaking open, then you close your heart in the name of comfort and control, even in the name of enlightenment.

Give up every idea of detachment, and experience your attachment fully. Experience the pain and the beauty of attachment, and the grief as what you are attached to is ripped away. Then you will recognize what can never be detached, what is not some stoic, unfeeling, unemotional, inhuman existence, but what is freely and consciously all of it.

# LETTING THE WORLD INTO YOUR HEART

## 49

n this time of global distress, with the threat of terror and the actuality of war, individual awakening is increasingly urgent. It is not just a good thing to do, or an addition to our knapsack of experience trinkets. It is not even about some kind of personal pleasure or achievement. Awakening is essential if we are to recognize the patterns of hatred and blame that go on within our own minds, and which, in turn, are reflected into the world. We can't wait for anyone else to stop. Our own projections have to stop.

We each have the power to stop the cycle of war projected both inward and outward. We each have the power to stop any remnants of the battle between ego and superego, my religion and your religion, my color and your color, my gender and your gender.

Most anyone reading this book is *extremely* privileged to not face imminent starvation, bombing, torture, or exile. That privilege can be used to stop the cycle of inner and outer torture. We each have the opportunity to stop the endless cycle of our personal stories—"Yeah, I'm really lucky, but what about what I don't have? What about what I could have? Why did they treat me that way? Why doesn't he treat me the way I want him to? Why are *they* causing all this trouble?"

With direct experience, any habitual belief can disappear in less than a second. Yet the familiar habits, hopes, deflections, and distractions somehow mysteriously arise again and again. They may have a horrendous momentum, but that momentum is slowed and then stopped with the force of consciousness.

I am often asked, "Why, why do the old habits continue to arise? How is it possible?" The why and how are because the seductive power of hope is still present: "If I just follow it *this* time, it will be perfect, just the way I want it to be. He or she will love me, I will love them, they will always treat me right, I will always treat them right, the world will be at peace, everybody will be happy, everybody will be fed. I will just follow this pattern one more time."

The invitation to stop is absolutely radical, and stopping is absolutely effortless. You can stop, *right now*. You can take full responsibility for the recognition of what is already unconditionally at peace within you right now. Nothing is needed from the past, the present, or the future to augment that peace. You can accept the responsibility to be true to that—not as a theory, an abstraction, or more mental punishment. Simply surrender the mind to peace. The possibility of surrender can be found in whatever emotion, circumstance, fear, or hope is appearing, without resorting to the habitual pattern of making war with it.

I invite you to take the world into your heart right now, not tomorrow when you have done something more, but now. In this very moment, you no longer have to try to figure out how to fix the world or your patterns. I am asking you to find the willingness to take the *totality* into your heart, to see if your heart has a limit.

What struck me after September 11, when the subsequent bombing began in Afghanistan, and then the U.S. went to war in Iraq, was that there were moments when people's hearts were broken so profoundly that they were open. There was a deepening of compassion, a deepening of the understanding of the absurd insult of the innocent being killed all over the world, in all cultures. Sadly, because these moments were so intense, and because people generally identify themselves as separate entities, most closed themselves off again from vulnerability and openness and went back to business as usual. But that business as usual is the business of individual suffering, the individual story of "me and my needs and who didn't meet them."

When you experience "other" as self, you experience deep pain and hurt. And you choose to either close to that or open even more. When you recognize there is no other, the pain of the world that you have denied is experienced as the pain of your own self. You can invite that universal pain into your heart. Then that very pain is revealed to hold the treasure, to hold the reality of the deepest, most profound truth. We *think* that the realization of truth is all about lightness, bliss, and ecstasy; but if that were so, realization would not include all. True realization is the doubtless certainty that you and *all* can never really be separated.

Are you ready to experience the naked, raw truth of the fragility of life forms and how quickly they can end, unexpectedly, even horribly, and the suffering that reverberates from that ending? To directly experience that fragility and suffering is to welcome the whole truth. To accept the invitation is to be still in whatever is arising and to tell the truth about what remains permanently here, in peace and in love.

In this moment in time, we can finally recognize how much is unknown politically, economically, culturally, and globally. We can seize the opportunity to meet that unknown-ness and discover the indefinable fulfillment that is forever unknowable.

Never in the history of the world have so many people been aware of what is happening on the other side of the globe while it is happening. Never have so many people been aware that the pattern of war is not new. And never have so many people been willing to say, "Stop."

Wherever you find yourself, you are invited at this moment to stop and recognize the sublime truth of who you are. This truth can always be found in surrendered unknowingness, but it is often covered by the concept of *me* or *mine*. The choice, then, is to be true to truth or to turn from it once again.

You can actually experience the fullness of peace in this moment, here, right now, regardless of circumstances. You can discover the joy that includes pain, the love that includes hate, the peace that includes war.

# THE CULT OF SOCIETY 50

O ften, as self-recognition approaches and the heart begins to deeply open, terror arises. This is the terror of being misused during a time of such profound vulnerability. Of course, this fear is based on past experiences of having been misused when vulnerable, the fear that if you are really open, you could be brainwashed and steered into some kind of dangerous or cultish behavior.

The reason this fear can arise so strongly is that you already have a very strong experience of being brainwashed and used in cultish behavior. This cult is called "society," and its cult-ure gives rise to suffering. If you look closely, everything that is associated with cult behavior can likewise be found in society's behavior. The same means of control are used: the constant reinforcement that you are helpless without society, that you cannot survive without obeying its rules, and that you will go to hell if you don't obey the tenets of its religion. This is the pervading societal condition.

The search for freedom often leads to a swing from one cult, family, church, or society, to another, smaller cult, subculture, church, or society. Eventually, we recognize that the new cult is just the same old thing, the same play all over again. From that disillusionment, cynicism can arise. Yet, even in cynicism, most of us still don't notice that we are, in fact, being misused every day. Whatever your attention is focused on, that is what is using you. It is a revealing exercise to see where your attention is in a day. Obviously, since you are in a body, some attention must go to its survival. This is natural biological conditioning that provides for bodily survival. That's fine. There is no need to stop that. Providing food, clothing, exercise, and shelter for the body is a legitimate use of attention. It is an imperative for the human life form. But even after the body has been fed, how much attention is still put into feeding it more, or feeding it better, or thinking about feeding it again? How much attention is put obsessively on clothing, on exercising, on finding your place in society? How much attention is paid to conjuring up all possible threats to future food, clothing, and shelter? If this is where your attention is, this is how your life is being used.

It is also true that wherever your attention is, this is what you love. True attention is not separate from love. What are you paying attention to? What do you love? You know you love to feel good. You know there are people whom you love. You love beautiful days. You love peace. But, if you delve a little deeper, you can see where your subconscious attention is, and you can tell the truth that you also love that.

This kind of investigation can be shocking, of course. It can reveal some old story of pain or loss or abuse. But this is a necessary shock. The attachment, the love of your identification as someone who has something or lacks something, must be recognized. All distractions of past or future keep false identifications in place.

It is extremely useful to discover where your attention goes, what it is you love. Even if it is a sick, masochistic, torturous love, a love that gives no rewards, a love that is miserable, you can finally tell the truth about it. In telling the truth, perhaps you will finally be able to pay full attention to that misery, rather than believing you love one thing while secretly giving attention to another. Telling the truth allows you to bring both things together. This is true, absolute, full inquiry into what is: an inquiry closer than any positive or negative emotion, any thought, or any circumstance.

Many people are concerned that at the end of their life, they will look back and see that it has all been useless. I salute this concern. If your life is to be of use, it must be investigated as if this day was the last day of your life. What has your body, your lifetime, your individual consciousness been about? How have they been used? The very willingness to see what cultish behavior is being either indulged or denied is the willingness to be ruthlessly honest. This can then reveal the possibility of seeing what remains permanently free in the face of everything.

Many people want to escape immediately into the bliss of the truth of freedom. You can, of course, since it takes less than a second to see the freedom that is always here. But I have seen that most minds then take that moment of truth and fold it into the prison of ego.

If, in some moment of grace, you have glimpsed the peace, limitlessness, and beauty of your being, I suspect that the reason you are reading this book is that you want permanence instead of just a glimpse. You want to realize that beingness is *always* here, not just in a moment of bliss. I also suspect that your mind has taken that glimpse and made it into something that you think you can make a part of your life and use as you like. You may have had a glimpse of beauty and the truth of freedom, and then had the thoughts arise: "How can I use this? How can I make this mine? How can I keep this? How can I forever be enlightened, self-realized, and happy?"

The truth is, your mind cannot *use* freedom. Freedom is free. It will never be bound. It will never be caught. Your mind will never catch it. Your mind will never make truth do its bidding. You can imagine you have caught it, you can imagine you are making it do your bidding, but it will prove itself free. Just wait and see.

You can, however, let the truth of freedom use your mind. You can let it keep your mind by surrendering your attention to what has been revealed as the source of all attention. Truth is bigger than what you can use. It is free of societal cult, religious cult, or culture of any kind.

So, then, what do you do about this fear of letting go of control? Nothing. You let that fear appear in the stillness of your being. When thought arises to distract attention from the vulnerability, return to the vulnerability itself. Don't attempt to conquer it. Be fully, purely vulnerable. The willingness to stop running and fully meet your fear of vulnerability is the same as the willingness to meet both the fear of death and the fear of freedom.

The fear of freedom is the fear of meeting the truth of who you are, the fear of this huge force that your mind cannot own, control, or even direct. Finally, the fear of anything is the fear of death, and as you already know, the fear of death is the same as the fear of life.

Most people first come into the spiritual subculture to escape the cult of the family or the cult of society. Yet, within each spiritual subculture, the tendency to make a cult based on the spiritual family or its particular teachings is always present. The same dramas, plays, villains, heroes, and projections arise, only now they are cloaked in spiritual garb.

It is possible, right now, wherever you find yourself, to stop. For this moment at least, turn your attention to where your life comes from. Shift your attention back to your life's source, to what gives your life the power to be aware, and to where your life goes when it is finished.

Everything in the conditioned mind will arise to deny the truth of freedom's presence. When freedom awakens, all the fixations and habits of your mind arise to pull you back under the control of those same fixations, habits, and conditioning. The power of the mind is awesome in its strength and subtlety, but where does that strength of mind get its power? What is the source of the individual mind? The mind cannot enclose that source with concepts, but the heart can realize it without a doubt.

If your attention is on the source of yourself, you realize a freedom that is beyond the onslaught of any conditioning that may appear. Then you are free of the compulsive need for safety and protection. You are free of habitual hatred, and you are free of prescribed adorations. You simply are.

# FREEDOM IS
# FACING DEATH 51

There are all kinds of deaths. There is the death of every moment. There is the death that occurs every night when you drop off into sleep, the death of a relationship ending, and the death when a child leaves home. But the death I would like you to turn your attention to now is physical death, the end of your physical life form.

In Western culture, the inevitable death of the body is usually avoided, denied, or artificially dressed up in some way. In that avoidance, the treasure that death reveals is lost. In your willingness to experience the certainty of your own death, true self-inquiry is possible.

As you are reading this, you have the privilege right now to actually consider the end of your life. You can put aside all physical and mental rituals and strategies that construct your life, and meet the reality of the end of your life. In this moment, you can stop everything and inquire deeply and truly into who you are, as if death were imminent. You can take this time to actually reflect on what your life has been about, on what is important and what is not. You can speak honestly to yourself. In this moment, you have no reason to lie.

The spiritual path is actually a path of death, a path of loss. Many people begin the spiritual search looking for attainment, but true spiritual attainment is revealed through the loss of everything. If you can investigate the loss of your life now, before death comes to take it, you have the possibility of dying freely, in peace, losing something very precious, yes, but gaining more in the capacity to meet the loss head-on.

The presence that animates your form is the same presence that animates all form. After the death of the body, that presence remains. Waking up to yourself as that presence results from the willingness to meet the death of every form, including your own. Everybody will die, just as the planet will someday die, just as all thought, all emotion, and all experience die.

As the body ages, the truth of death becomes more and more apparent. No matter what you might do to preserve the body's health, energies are lost and unrecoverable. Finally, the irrevocable truth is that the body will die. The sooner this can be faced, the greater the possibility of realizing what remains, free of death.

Since most of us humans have identified ourselves as individual bodies, death becomes the event to be avoided at all costs, even at the cost of our integrity and souls. I invite you to look within your life right now. See if you have sold your integrity and soul for some notion of survival of the body. This is basically what the desire to be "good" is about. You desire to be good so that nobody will hurt you, so that you will fit in, so that your body will survive. The same can be said about the desire to be knowledgeable or attractive. This is why it is also important to fully experience your own badness, your own stupidity, and your own ugliness. You must experience the polarities that are at the core of your conditioning. Just after you have the thought "I am somebody," some variation on the thought "I am somebody *good*" or "I am somebody *bad*" arises. Your heart of hearts knows that both are lies. In this knowing, you can honestly inquire, "Without the body, without the qualities of goodness or badness, without the feelings, without the thoughts, who am I?"

I invite you now, this moment, to die before your body dies, to recognize your attachment to your body, and to face its inevitable end. And in this facing, to tell the truth about who you really are. If you are willing to stop for one moment and face death, you will have some time to see what life is like when you have met the reality of the death of form. What is the experience of life when there is no "you" left? What is the experience of problems when they are not "your" problems?

To meet our death while the body is still alive is counterintuitive, contrary to our conditioning as organisms designed to avoid pain and fear. We normally listen to fear because it is part of the survival mechanism of the human body. There is nothing wrong with that. But self-inquiry takes the mind deeper than what is right for survival. Once the desire arises to truly be free, the question of what survives after the body dies is more important than simply surviving. Then we can meet death.

Am I talking about suicide? No! To meet death is not suicide, nor is it the least bit dangerous. It only seems dangerous. What is dangerous, what is a living suicide, is to live your life in bondage to the belief that you are limited to a body. As long as you resist the fact of death and hide from death through the tricks of the mind, you will suffer. In the recognition that death is simply the cessation of all experience, you can actually invite death *now*.

Who are you? Are you a body? Teachers tell you that you are radiant consciousness, that you are the light, the truth, but you must recognize who you are for yourself. Otherwise, whatever anyone says is just another addition to the story of who you believe yourself to be. *True, lasting recognition is not just an addition to a collection of spiritual experiences.*

Do you have the courage to be who you truly are, to die to your conditioning? This is a huge question that should only be answered with serious examination.

You cannot live fully until you are willing to die fully; and you cannot die fully until you are willing to meet the fear of death fully. If you really meet the fear of death, you are at peace. You recognize what cannot die. I am not speaking of reincarnation, because the hope that you will reincarnate is still rooted in a fear of death.

I invite you to ask yourself the questions that are really the heart and core of all true self-inquiry: *What is it that dies when the body dies? Who is it that dies? Who is asking these questions?* Inquire deeply into yourself. Look closer and closer.

Experience the energy, attention, and effort that it takes to keep death away. Are you aware of the fear of being nothing, of no longer existing? Right now, let your consciousness sink into the core of that fear. Let yourself be nothing right now. All is finished. All is over. What is left? What remains when every*thing* is gone? Who are you?

# THE SERIOUSNESS OF YOUR INTENT 52

E veryone, at some point in their life, has been mysteriously, luckily, touched by the power of grace, whether they recognized it in that moment or not. The moment that you recognize it, you think, "My God, what grace!" Maybe before that moment, you only knew grace as a concept, but when you experience it, it is alive and real. The Holy Spirit is alive and real, and you know it because you have been touched by it. That moment of grace is a mystery. There is nothing you could have done to deserve it. Perhaps you believe it to be a predestined moment in a predestined lifetime in which you have been selected by grace. Yet, in my years of speaking with people—and I have been to both prisons and churches, and have met with both intellectuals and the uneducated—I have found that grace leaves its mark everywhere, with no apparent concern for karma, religious practice, accomplishment, or intellectual understanding.

If you know you have been touched by grace, you are wise to assume that you could not fully deserve it. Now what is your responsibility? What is the responsibility of individual consciousness to the absolute consciousness that has made itself known through grace? How do you respond?

I sometimes refer to this responsibility as the "seriousness of your intent"—the intent to break through conditioned existence, to realize true freedom, to surrender fully to the power and the force of grace. I don't mean "seriousness" as something humorless or heavy. The intention to realize true freedom is definitely joyous, but it is not trivial. If it is trivial, then there is no possibility of breaking through conditioned ignorance. When grace or freedom is just another *thing*, there is no possibility of unwinding egoic identification.

With the serious intention to truly be free comes the recognition that nothing is more important than freedom. Nothing. Not pleasures, health, relationships, accomplishments, or understanding. And when nothing is more important, the waves of the mind part, and conditioned existence loses its hold.

The only hold conditioned existence has is the importance that your mind gives it. Giving importance to conditioned existence means continuing to pursue all that you have *learned* you need to be happy, whether that involves mental learning, conditioned emotions, or physical instincts. If any of that is more important than the desire to be completely free, then your response to grace is less than complete. You will, of course, dip into the ocean of peace and freedom. You will have wonderful experiences, magical experiences, experiences of ecstasy and bliss, but you will never have full and complete self-recognition until your intention is one hundred percent.

If you are drawn to the fullness, the completeness, and the totality of the freedom you have glimpsed, if this is more important than dipping into personal pleasure and power, then the seriousness that is demanded must be the priority of your life. If it is not, then conditioned desires will retain their power.

We have both latent and blatant ideas of what will make us happy. Even though grace may reveal itself as the purity and joyousness of our true nature, we have a tendency to cling to our learned desires. I have heard it time and again: "Yes, I want freedom, I really want freedom, *and* I really want a good relationship, I want a beautiful place to live, I want financial security ..." Please understand that there is nothing wrong with these desires. But if what you really want is freedom, recognize that any desire other than the desire for freedom will bleed attention from the potential for realizing freedom in this moment.

If you want truth to give you some thing, it is not truth you want; it is the thing you want, and that thing has everything to do with power, sex, or survival, the three matrices of bodily desire.

Maybe the promise of the thrill of some kind of personal enlightenment has brought you to the door of inquiry. But if you find that door still closed, it is time to tell the truth. Waking up to your true nature promises to give you nothing. In wanting only to wake up, you find everlasting freedom, joy, and the bliss of being.

Tell the truth about what you want, what you are seeking under the guise of enlightenment or self-realization. Profoundly examine your motivation: What are you really, seriously intent upon? What you find can be humbling. If you discover pockets of intent that have nothing to do with freedom, truth, or God, then you have a choice to shift attention to freedom. If, in fact, you want to hold on to something a little bit longer in the arenas of power, sex, and survival, if you want to milk a little more pleasure from *things,* then tell the truth. There is a moment of truth that is profound, where, if you truly want freedom, you are willing for your whole life to end right now. You are not waiting another moment. Only truth is important. This is seriousness of intent.

# INTENTION AND SURRENDER 53

T he intention to be free can lead you home through the worst hells, even through a lifetime of hell. The intention itself is the light that says, "Home is here." It is not an ordinary intention, having to do with some desire to get something; it is of an altogether different order. It is the truest teacher in your life. It asks you to give over your self-hatred, your hatred of others, your blaming, justifying, grasping, and rejecting to the intention to be free.

You can spend much of your life resisting the call of freedom, fighting it, running from it, denying it, disbelieving it, or imagining it to be unimportant. This resistance is the crux of your suffering.

Astonishingly, your intention creates the clarity to see, or seek help with, your particular habits of suffering. That clarity brought you to this point, and it will take you where you need to go next. To trust that intention is to trust life. How you make use of the people who appear in your life, as well as the circumstances, thoughts, emotions, and contradictions, is up to you. You have absolute and complete choice. I do not mean this as another New Age version of "I am choosing to create my reality." I mean choosing how your current reality can be used by your intention to be free.

A glimpse of the true nature of your being is like a kiss from the divine. The kiss itself is a mystery of grace. There is nothing *you* could have done to *create* it. Rather than bow at the feet of this blessing, you often form a plan to take it and "create your reality" with it. Inevitably, any attempt to co-opt this blessing, even with the most altruistic intentions, will manifest yet another experience of the divine's slap—a necessary humbling of the newly inflated "enlightened" mind. If the slap itself is really surrendered to, then the blessing of the slap is just as deep as the blessing of the kiss. If it is truly surrendered to, you fall on your knees and give thanks for this slap. You give thanks for the exposure of the tendency to try to own truth, the tendency to try to possess what is always free. You will recognize that your life is blessed beyond belief.

It is also a common occurrence to want more of the sweet kiss and the bliss of freedom. When you are totally fulfilled, you are totally in love. And when you are totally in love, you do not say, "Well, I have had enough of love." Instead, you say, "More." But if the mind co-opts the love, then "more" is determined by an agenda, an image, or a plan of where more can be found. Love is free. Freedom is free. Where you look for more is where you found it to begin with, which is right here, wherever you are. There is always more *here,* because more *is* the space of your own openness.

We are trained to think that we know what we should be doing with the grace of the gift of self-recognition, this treasure of true freedom; here is where surrender and vigilance come into play. It feels safe to plan how to integrate it, channel it, or serve it in some way. But any plan is based on an idea that you know what to do with the vastness that has blown your concepts apart, and this is again the arrogance of the inflated ego.

Papaji often cited a quote from the writings of the Sufi poet Kabir, who said that he once experienced reality for fifteen seconds, and the rest of his life was spent in obedience to that.

The challenge is to surrender to not knowing how your life will be used, or even if your whole life will fall apart. The opportunity is to surrender to something much bigger than what you have called "your" life, to discover how "your" life can be a response to the invitation to live fully as a servant to freedom. Serving freedom is quite different from serving ideas of your freedom. Doing what *you* want because it makes you feel free is not the same as responding in service to what is free already. Surrender is the call from within to fully, absolutely realize yourself as freedom *itself.* The challenges are huge. They must be. Otherwise, we would trivialize this experience just as we have trivialized so many experiences of love. The surrender must be total. Anything less is a form of self-torture in the name of safety. Living fully as one, as all, is its own safety. The safety is in knowing that when this particular life form is finished, what it has served remains.

All you need is to trust the peace that is revealed and to be willing to discover freshly, at the core of each form of limitation, the boundless, limitless perfection of lasting peace and freedom. What remains when all else passes is trustworthy. If you trust thoughts, events, or people to give you safety, you will be disillusioned.

If you do not have an abiding recognition that you are already free, just as you are, wherever you find yourself, then your mind is still involved in a story. Maybe it is one of the deepest stories. To examine that story, you can inquire directly within: *What do I need to be free?*

Take a moment to consider the strong possibility, even the certainty, that all these stories are lies made up through the imaginative power of the mind. What if nothing is needed for freedom?

# CROSSING THE LINE INTO FREEDOM  54

False identification is exposed when life as it has been known is revealed not to be life as it *is*. Even if the experience of revelation lasts only a moment, you know it has changed your life forever. In this moment, you cross a line where you consciously know that your life is directed toward something more than what you knew before. That moment cracks open the very tightly woven story of a particular life and reveals it to be nothing in the face of the truth of life.

People on the spiritual path often spend much unnecessary time either trying to recapture a moment of truth or berating themselves because some personality trait, emotion, or behavior has reappeared. It is possible, however, to see all that appears in the context of the truth that was consciously glimpsed in a single instant.

The great mistake after the line has been crossed is in seeing anything that happens after that as somehow separate from that moment. If you are willing to hold all experience as present in that revelation, all the disgusting past habits and latent tendencies of the mind arise in the truth of what remains free and at peace. They are not something that contradicts or is separate from truth.

We have all spent time on self-negating thoughts and feelings, and in that, we discount the glimpse of grace. We emphasize what follows that glimpse as proof of having lost it, rather than recognize what follows as proof that nothing can be separate from the wholeness of truth.

When you recognize that this glimpse has changed your life forever, and you are willing to tell the truth about what is already here, then that glimpse can change it even more. It changes your concepts about your past, it changes your future, and, most important, it reveals what is changeless right here in the present. Then everything that arises, however difficult in the moment, is a conscious present-time discovery of truth. Then you see the play of personal identification for what it is—divine theatre—and everything in your life can be used in the service of a fresh discovery of truth. There is only one truth, one reality; everything else is simply entertainment for the mind. In any moment, you have the power to recognize, "Oh my God, I am actually getting very identified with this. I am now believing it to be the final reality."

If spirituality and the recognition of your true self were limited only to certain experiences, leaving out the vast majority of your experiences, what would be the point?

The question is: Can you live with all the ups and downs of the experience of being human, and still be conscious of, and nurtured by, the truth of who you are? *Yes!* This is not just for the sages of the past sitting on mountaintops. This is for you. Perhaps it took aeons for people sitting on mountaintops to develop reflective consciousness to such a degree that now you can actually open to receive what is finally and presently real. As I said before, this is a time of the ordinary awakening. You can see for yourself: "Here I am, identifying with whatever is bothering me, rather than being fully engaged in what is effortlessly present." At any time of the day, in a split second, you can simply check: "Has that which was revealed gone anywhere? What is the deeper truth in this moment?" This is vigilance.

If you are serious in your resolve to be vigilant, then your resolve will be tested. Once you consciously say, "Okay, I am ready. I am ready for everything to appear and test my confidence in what is true, what is real," then of course you will be thrown to the ground time and again. You are playing with the master, life itself.

You can expect re-identification to occur. If you expect re-identification, then the suffering that accompanies it reveals whatever arrogance, sleepiness, denial, or investment in some old story is still being indulged. Then you can find a continually deepening humbling that serves an even stronger resolve to vigilance.

This is the potential. This is the hugeness of the play of human existence. It makes your story seem very small. And it is! But the vastness of a life of true freedom defies measurement.

Right now, in this moment, who you are is eternal freedom. Everything that you imagine yourself to be arises in that freedom, exists in that freedom, and disappears back into that freedom. Freedom doesn't go anywhere. It didn't suddenly appear when you were born, and it doesn't disappear when you die. Freedom is the truth of life. Freedom is who you are. Not who you have named yourself; your name appears and disappears. Not who you have imagined yourself to be; that changes with time. Not who you feel yourself to be; that feeling comes and goes. Freedom is always here, and there is no end to it. Freedom is the essential nature of consciousness, and consciousness is the source of individual awareness.

If you can cross this line into conscious self-recognition, then everything that arises does so only to deepen it. Then the rest of your lifetime is lived in that recognition and in the celebration and sharing of it.

As a way of investigating any remaining boundaries to freedom, you can ask yourself this question: *Who or what tells me I am not free?* Again, there are no right or wrong answers. Some answers will be trivial, absurd, and mundane, while others may be earthshaking. It doesn't matter; just let them arise freely from the unconscious. The purpose is to expose the conditioned beliefs of the mind and to discover their reality or lack of reality.

Take a moment to reflect on, and perhaps to experience, your emotions and your body sensations with the thought I am not free. Experience the weight of that thought, the temptation of that thought, even the safety of that thought—the absurdity of that thought masquerading as reality.

Now experience the difference, the lightness, and the release generated with the thought I am free.

Then, behind both these thoughts, experience that which is aware of all thought. Recognize the inherent emptiness of thought, while also recognizing the pain or pleasure that the thought causes.

In this moment, ask yourself the question *Who am I?* If there is a thought that appears in response, let it go. Return to simple presence, simple awareness. Recognize what is always present in both thoughts of confirmation and thoughts of negation.

T he most important thing I can leave you with is vigilance. Vigilance is the resolve to be faithful to the truth of who you are: pure consciousness, free awareness. When you are vigilant, you do not believe the temptations of any thought that tells you that you are *only* a body with its particular needs, emotions, thoughts, and relations. Obviously, all bodies have particular needs, emotions, thoughts, and relations, but all particulars appear in the whole of who you are. If you allow your attention to sink into its source, then you see there is no problem with body, needs, emotions, and relations. It is all consciousness, all God. It is all *you*. Vigilance is the willingness to surrender in every moment to the truth that holds *all*.

When you invite vigilance into every moment of your life, then all concepts of "doing" vigilance are dropped. If you have an idea of vigilance as doing something, even in the slightest, then vigilance takes effort and cannot be "done" twenty-four hours a day. Recognize that vigilance is natural to awareness, and awareness is always present.

Vigilance *is* self-inquiry. Self-inquiry *is* vigilance. Neither is a mental exercise. Neither is a "doing."

Self-inquiry is alive. It is experiential. Rather than looking for a specific answer, it rests in an open-ended question, waiting for an answer.

Without hoping to achieve a particular state, but rather keeping an open-ended inquiry into what is here, ask yourself: *What is always here? What remains after everything that is passing through here is finished?* This questioning is the vigilance. There is no end to self-inquiry, just as there is no end to true freedom.

Life itself becomes the inquiry. Life itself becomes the teacher. A natural curiosity develops for investigating the true reality of everything that is passing through life. Whatever thought, emotion, or life circumstance is passing through, you can ask, "What is this?" You can allow your consciousness to delve all the way into it, and you will discover the familiar yet fresh spaciousness that *is* the inclusiveness of alive self-inquiry. Self-inquiry is not a practice separate from life, not a way to get somewhere other than here, but the discovery that truth is everywhere. To discover this freshly in every moment is vigilance.

Self-inquiry is not something that you learn to do. It is something that you learn you naturally *are.* You are awareness inquiring into itself and discovering itself everywhere, in formlessness and in every form.

In our evolution as a species, we have accumulated an enormous number of concepts about what it means to be free. Some of these concepts were useful at a certain point, but now they are only a burden. If you remain true to the accumulation of your concepts, then they will be your reality. In having the intention to tell the truth about the peace that is always present, you will realize true freedom ,and you can live your life as that freedom.

Throughout time, people have used spiritual understanding for ego-aggrandizement, so be aware that this kind of arrogance is likely to appear. It must appear. It is very humbling for it to appear. If you desire to keep spiritual arrogance away, then very subtly a denial mechanism will arise whereby you think, "My specialness is not arrogance; this is the choiceless truth." Vigilance is the awareness of that temptation arising, awareness of choosing to be *somebody* who has *something.* By recognizing arrogance, you hobble its power.

Yes, arrogance will appear. Let it appear so that the pain of it can be experienced and the lie of it can be exposed. Tell the truth. In your acceptance of the truth of who you are, you can allow that truth to guide your life. Then the support that *is* the vigilance is always with you as your own self, your own heart. Then there is a real possibility that this human experiment will not end in failure.

As pure consciousness, incarnated as human beings on this planet, we have the invitation to be completely responsible for where we find ourselves. If your intention is to be true to your mind, to being right, to knowing, then you will have enormous support for that. If your intention is to be true, period, then you will see that there is an even greater support, perhaps unseen and unknown, yet with a power that provides the courage to meet fully whatever appears. This support mysteriously reveals itself in living answer to your original prayer to return home to who you really are.

Wherever you find yourself, this is where you tell the truth. In each instance of telling the truth, a deeper truth is revealed. Finally, the choiceless truth of who you are is revealed to be permanently here, permeating everything. Not a *thing* and not separate from anything—the true radiance that was in your pocket all along.

The Gangaji Foundation offers public meetings and retreats with Gangaji, as well as books, audios, and videos. To receive a complete catalog and schedule of programs, please visit www.gangaji.org, email us at info@gangaji.org, or call us at 800.267.9205.